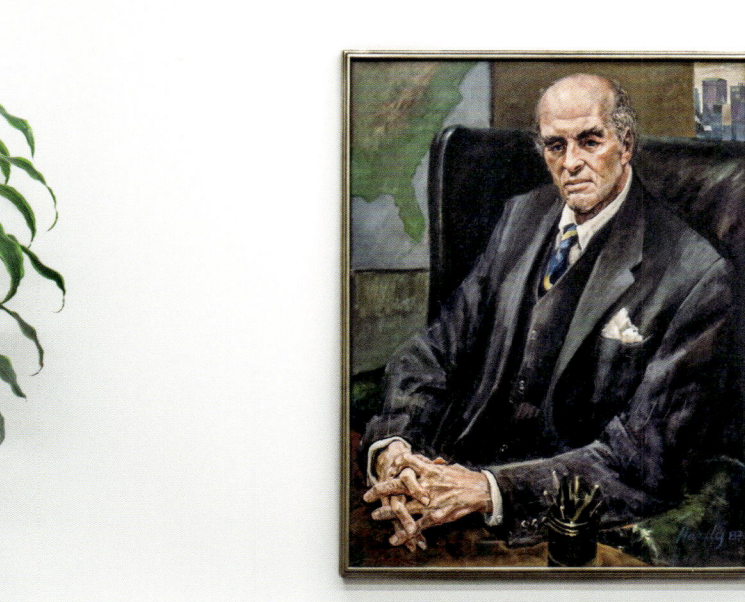

Cofounders: Taj Forer and Michael Itkoff
Creative Director: Ursula Damm
Copy Editor: Gabrielle Fastman

ISBN: 978-1-942084-99-0

Printed by Faenza Group SpA, Italy

Daylight Books
E-mail: info@daylightbooks.org
Web: www.daylightbooks.org

Robin L. Dahlberg

BILLABLE HOURS
in 6-minute increments

Daylight

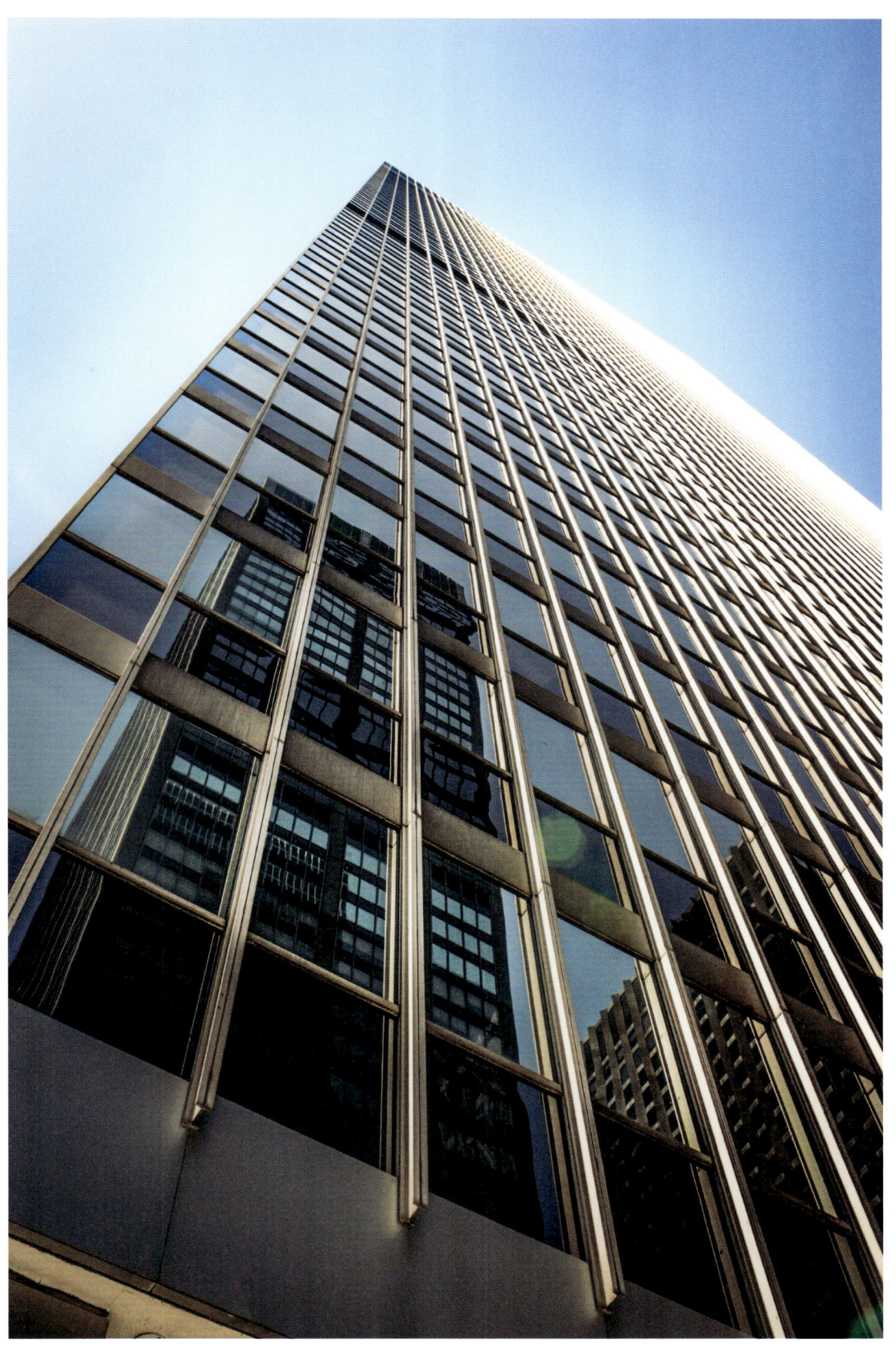

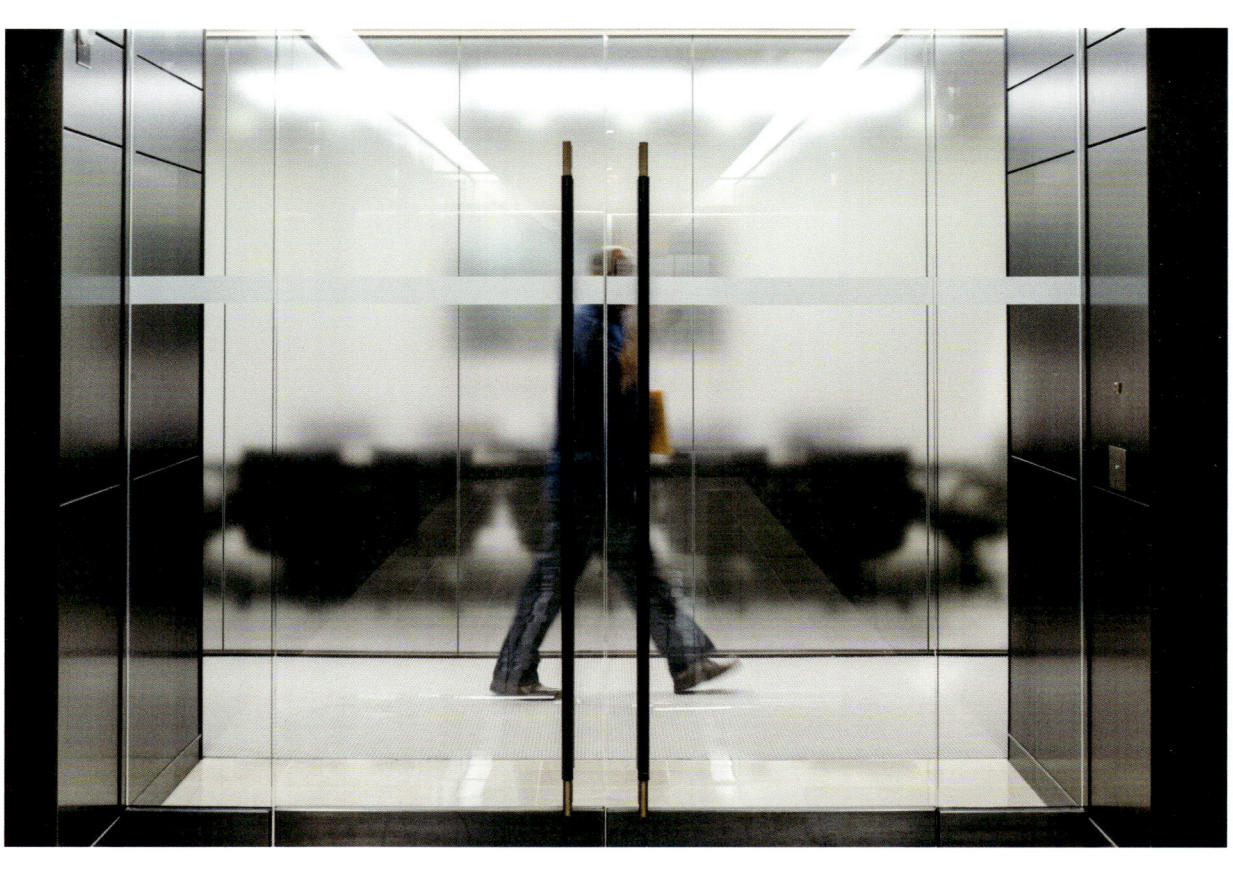

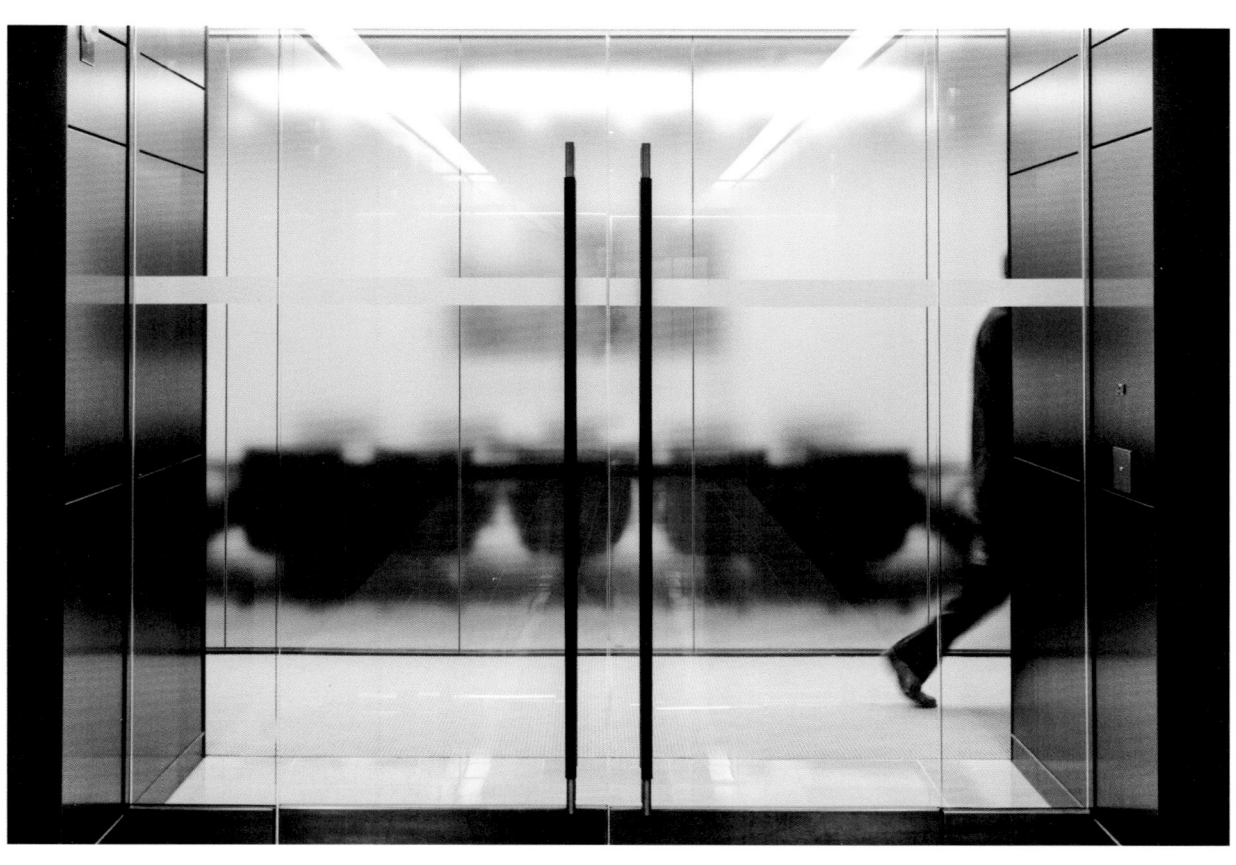

"Time is money."

—Benjamin Franklin

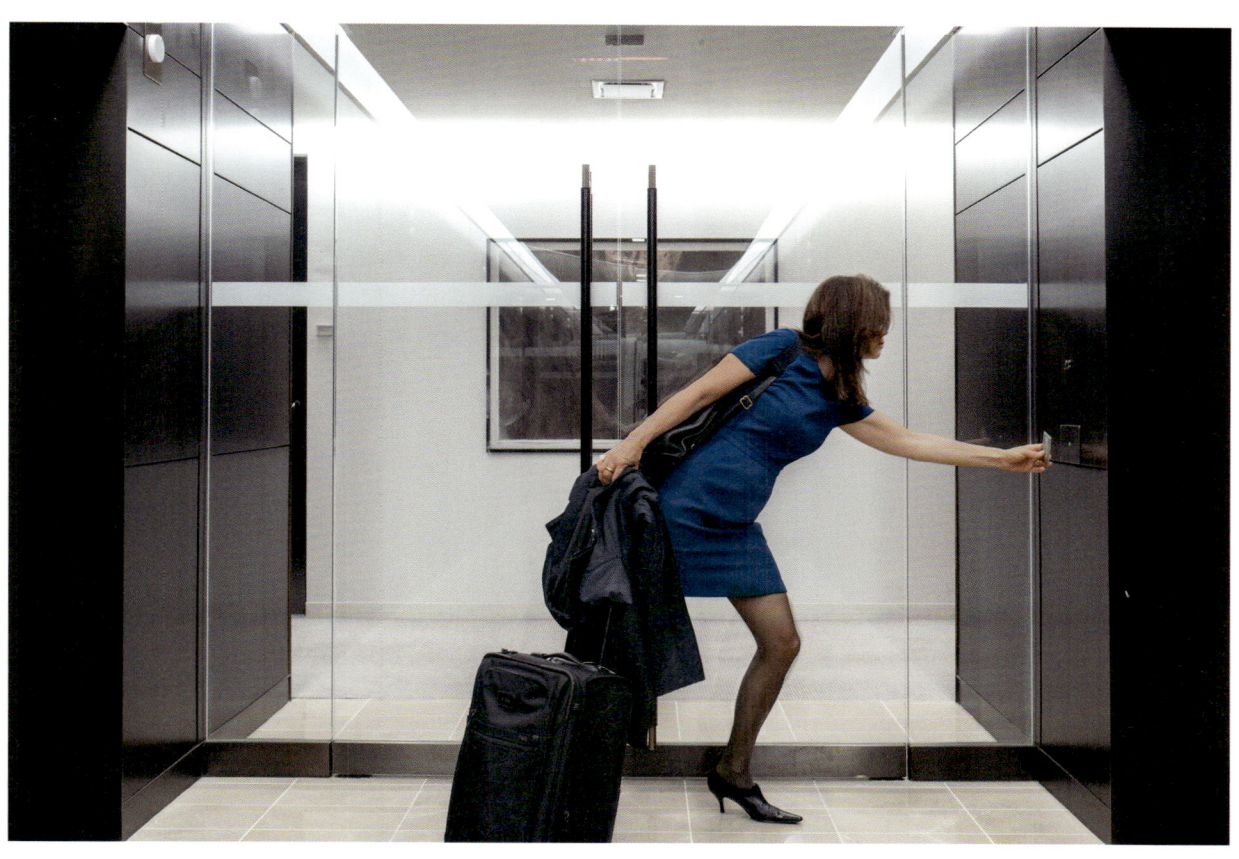

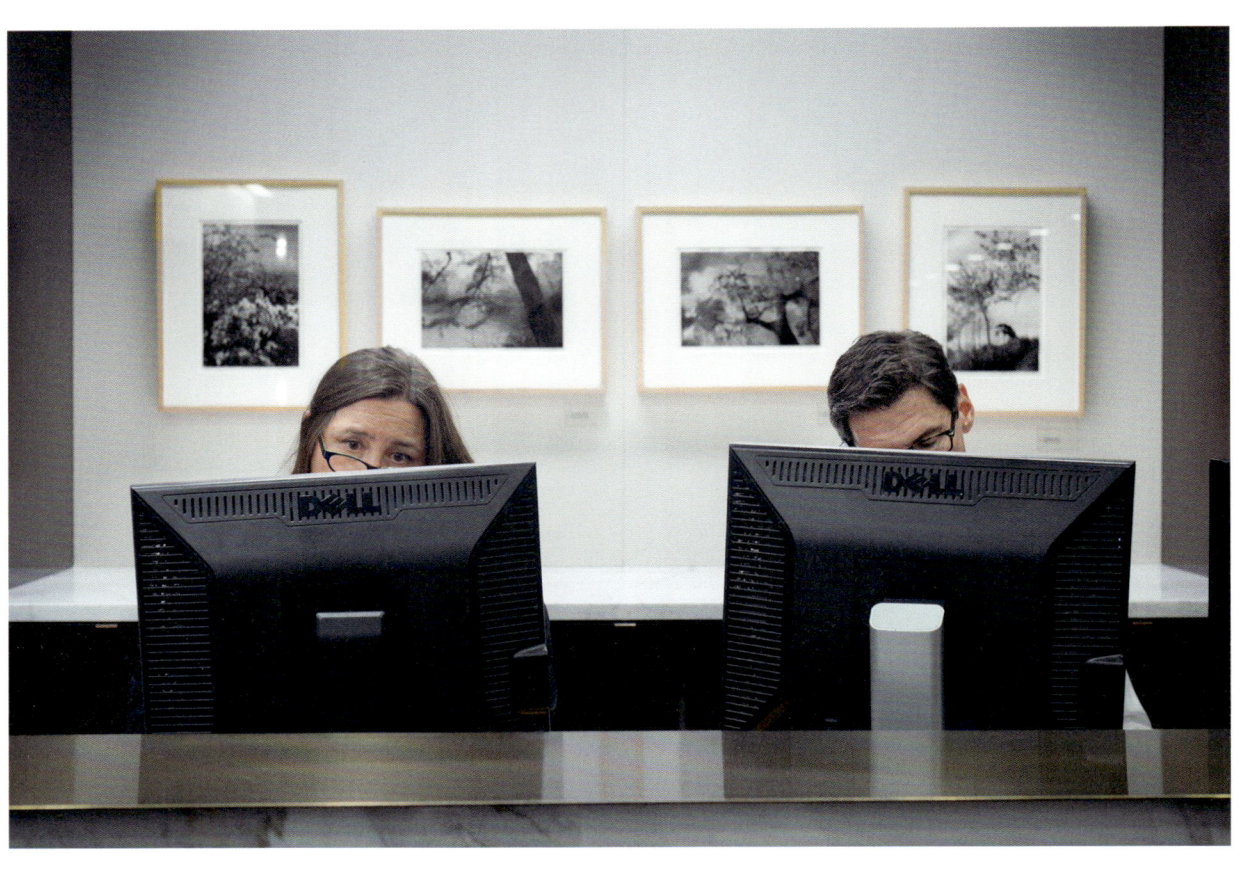

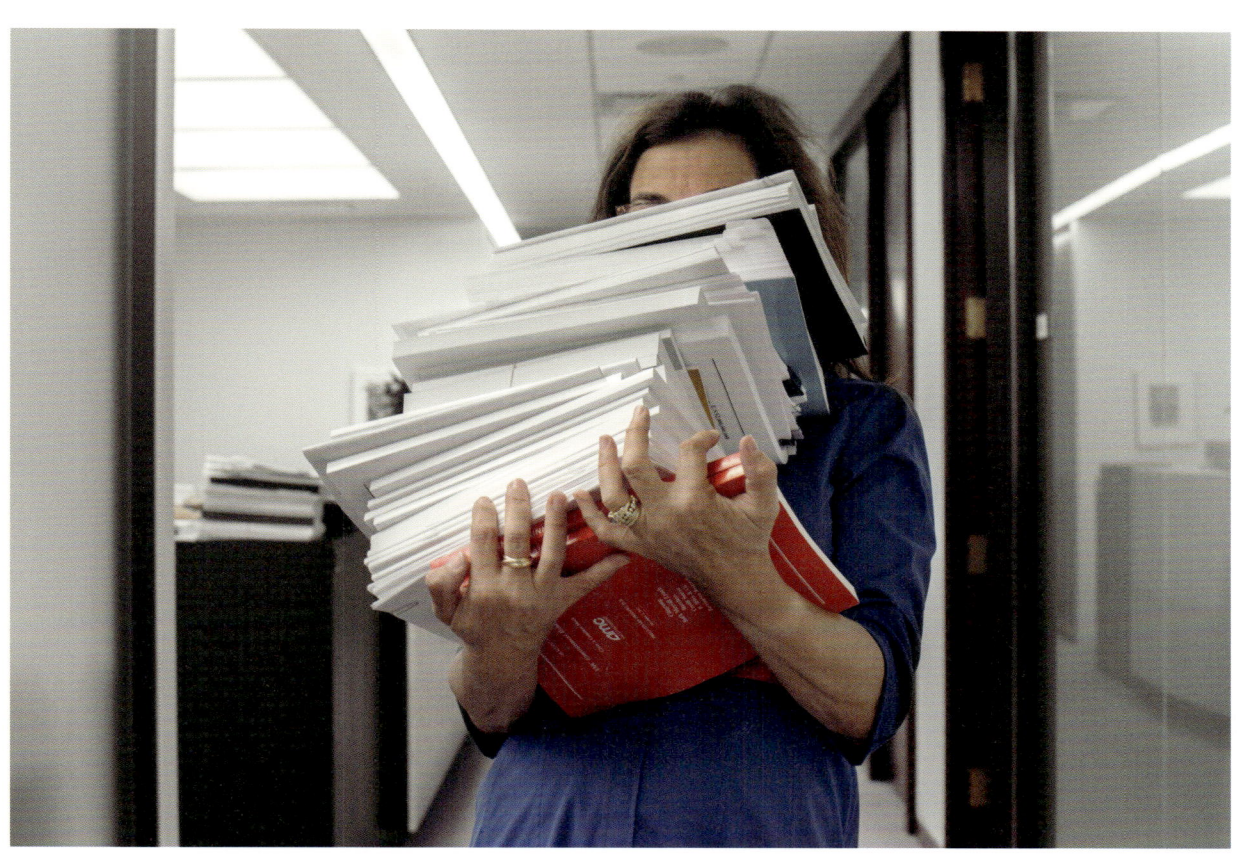

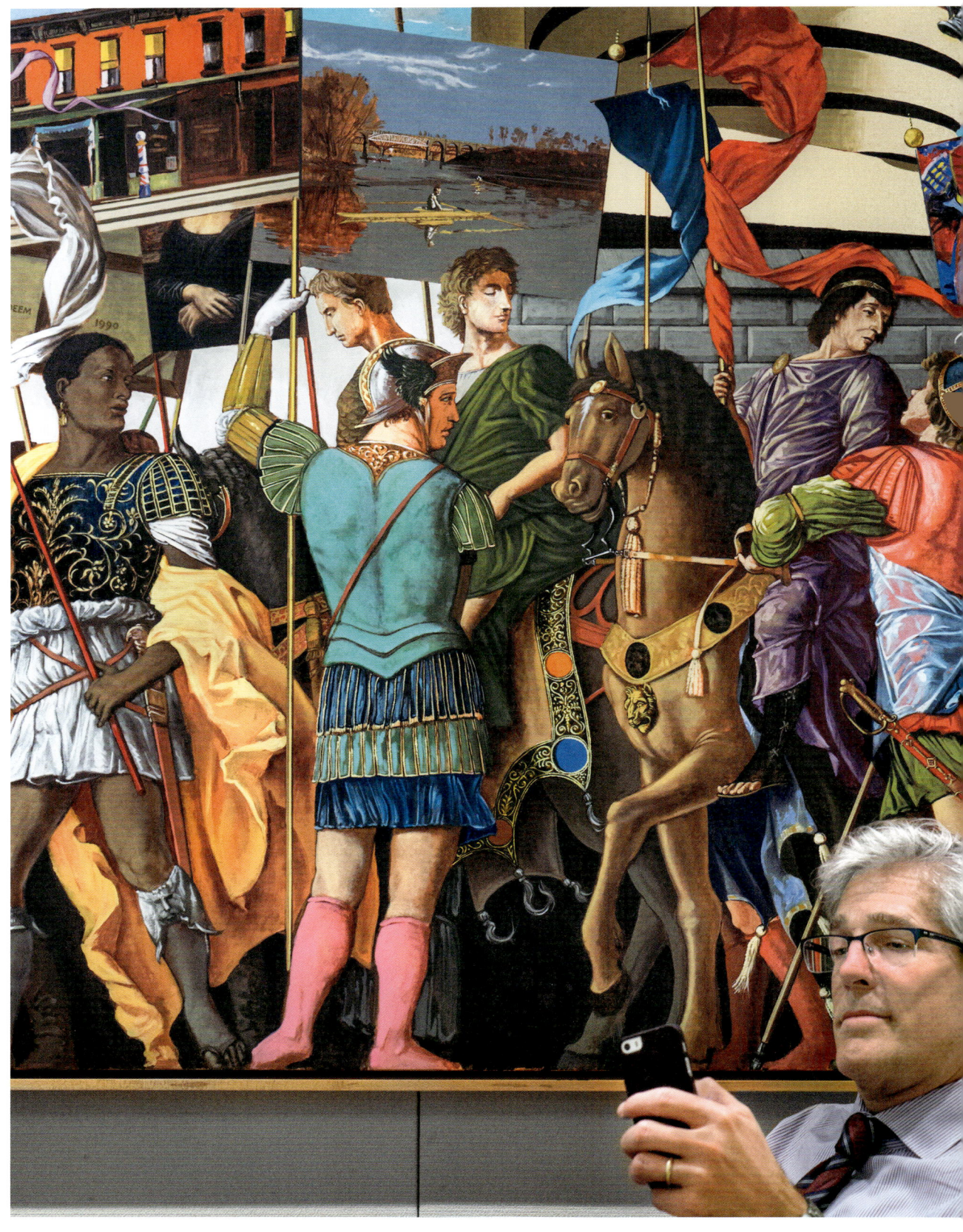

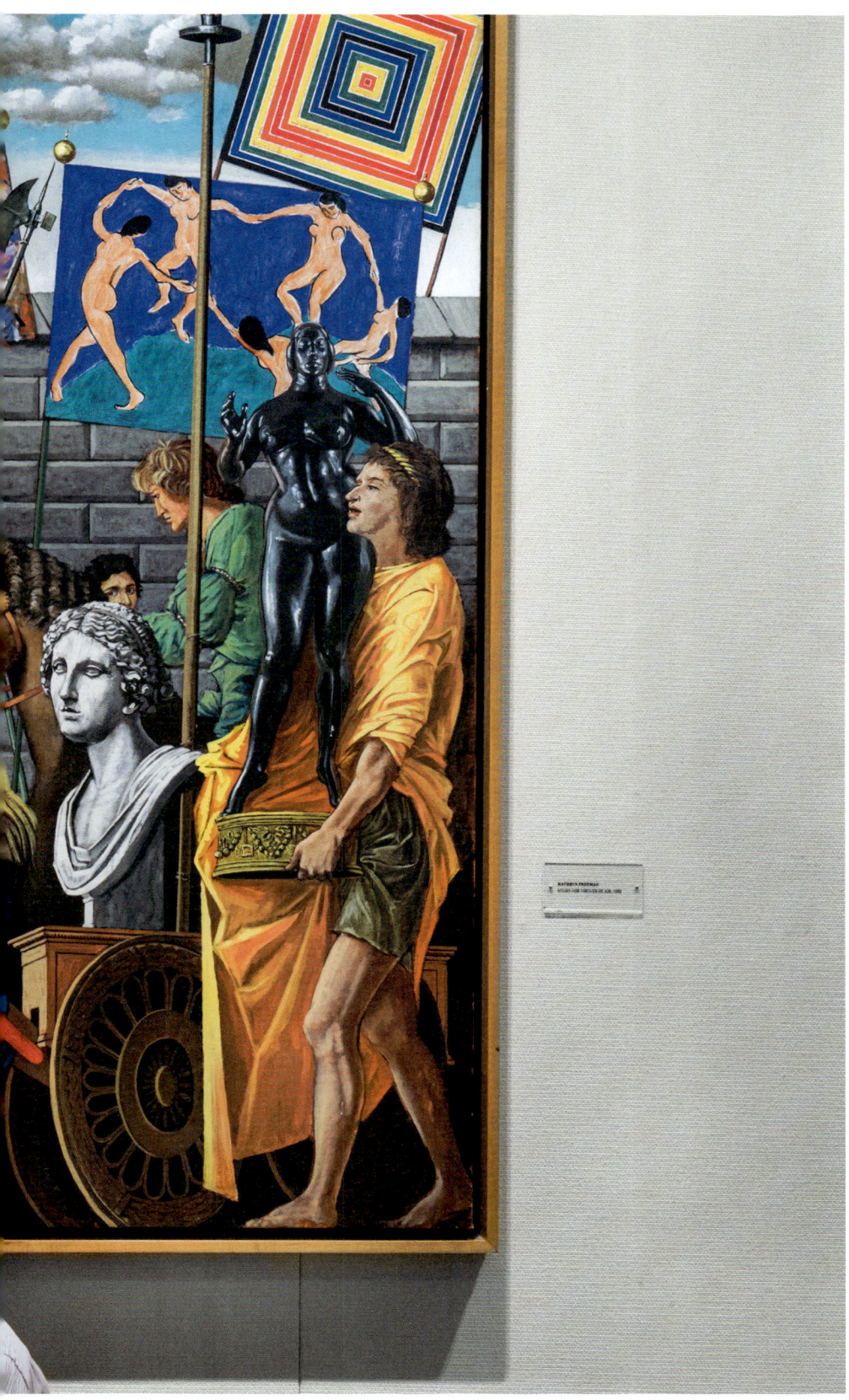

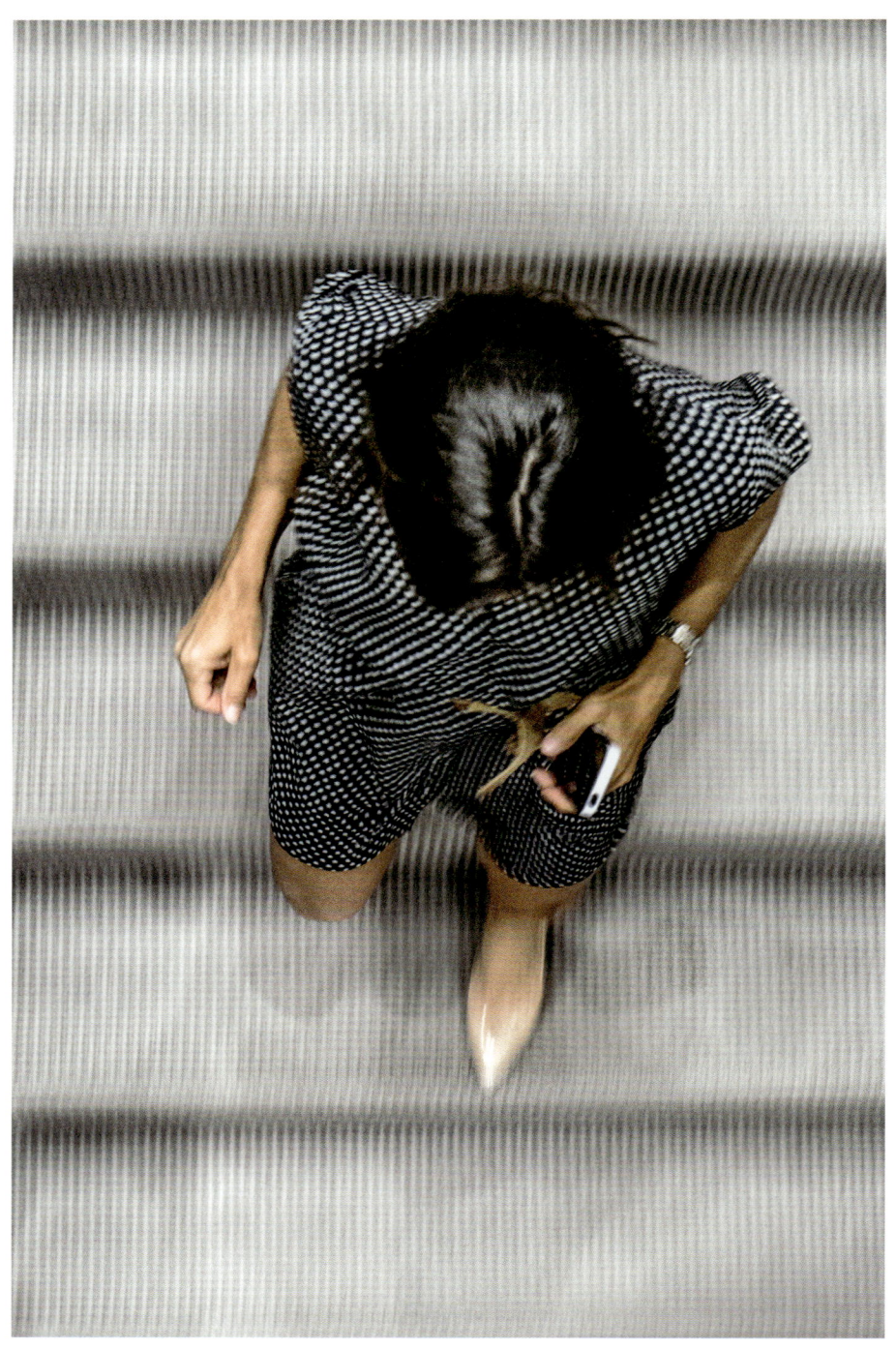

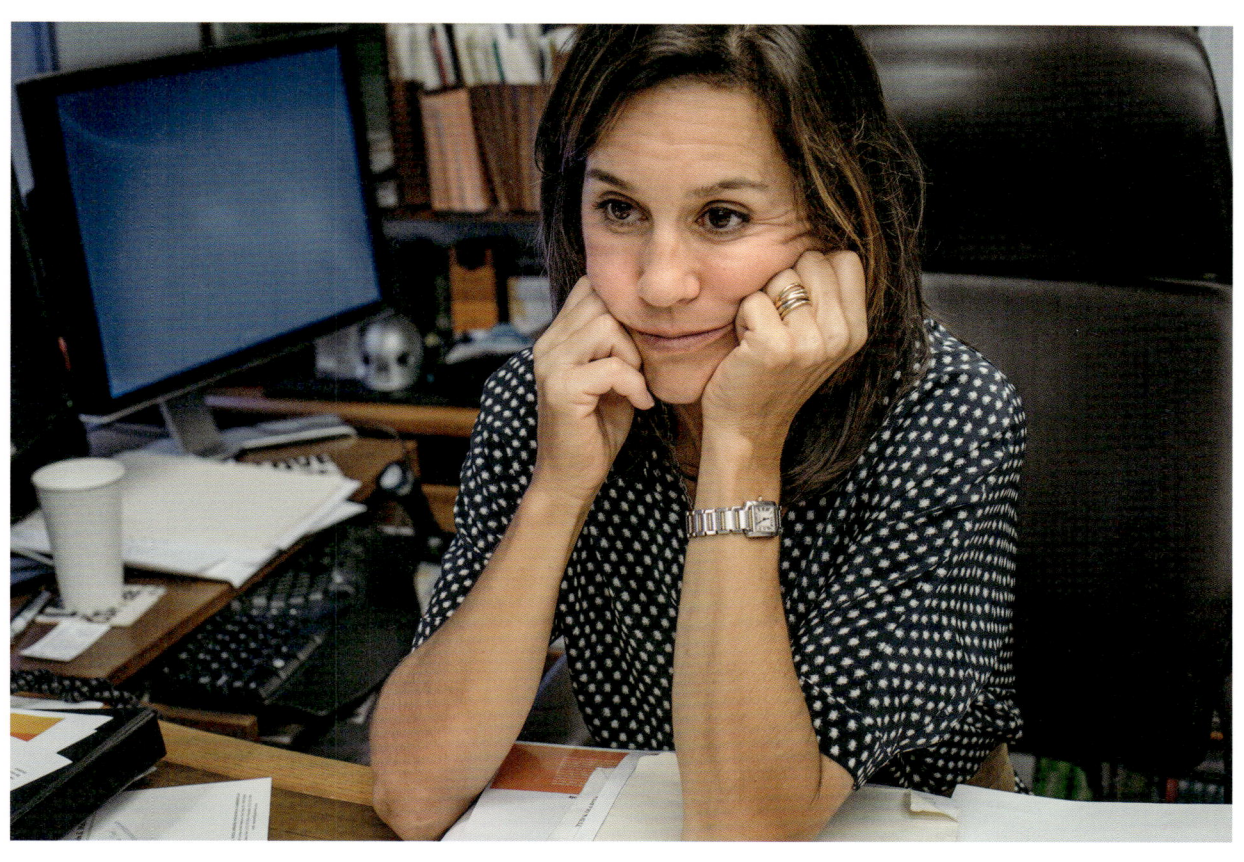

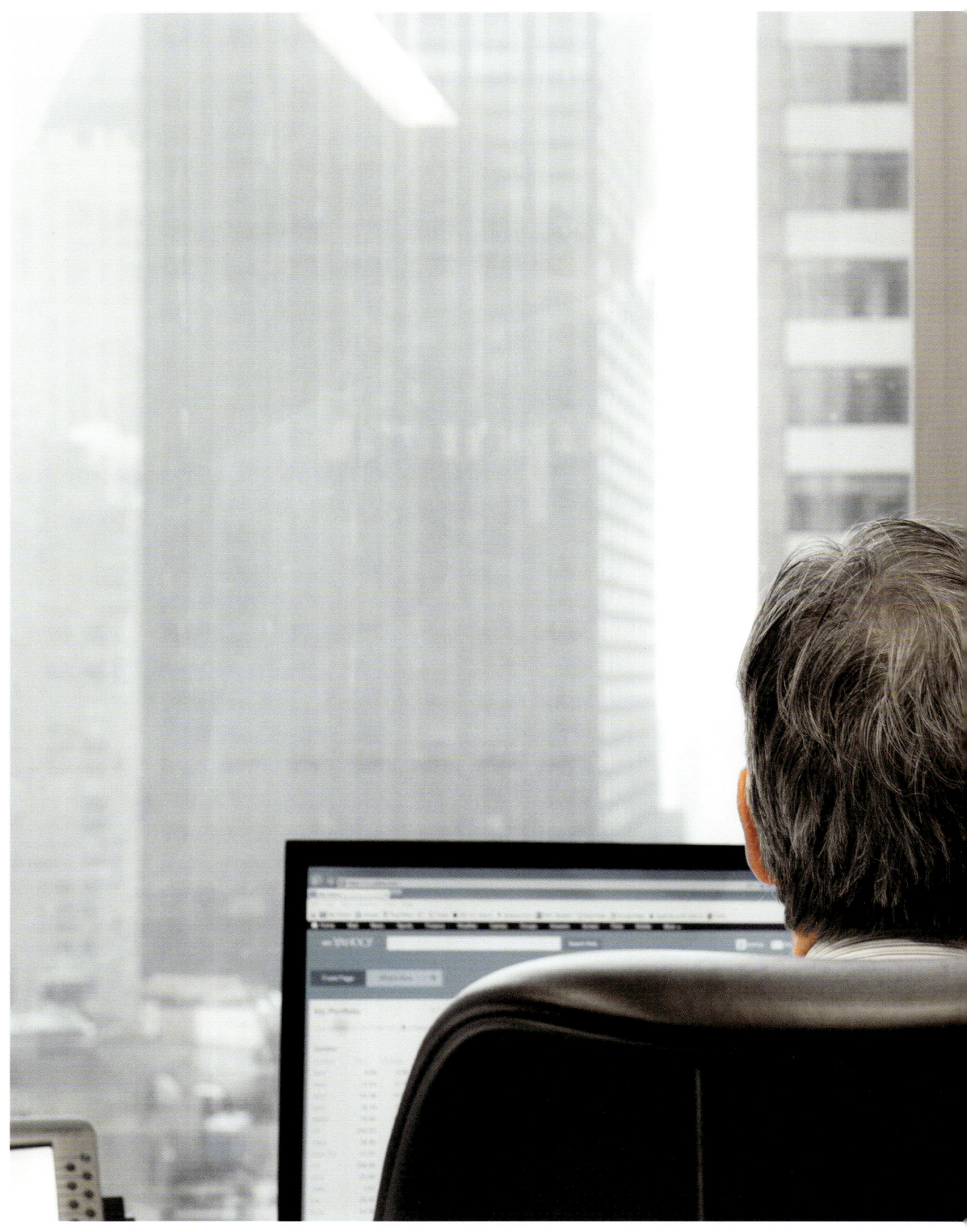

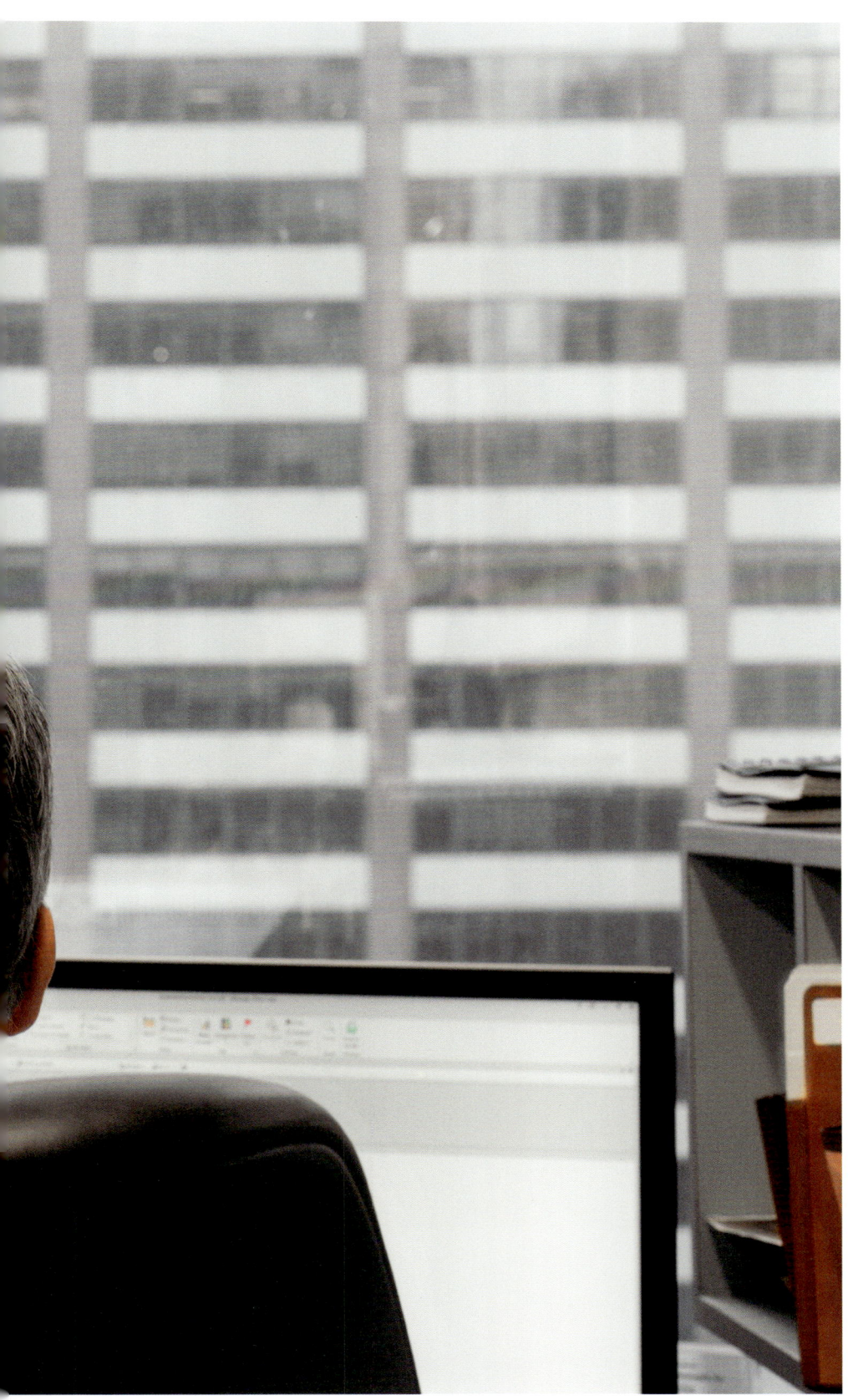

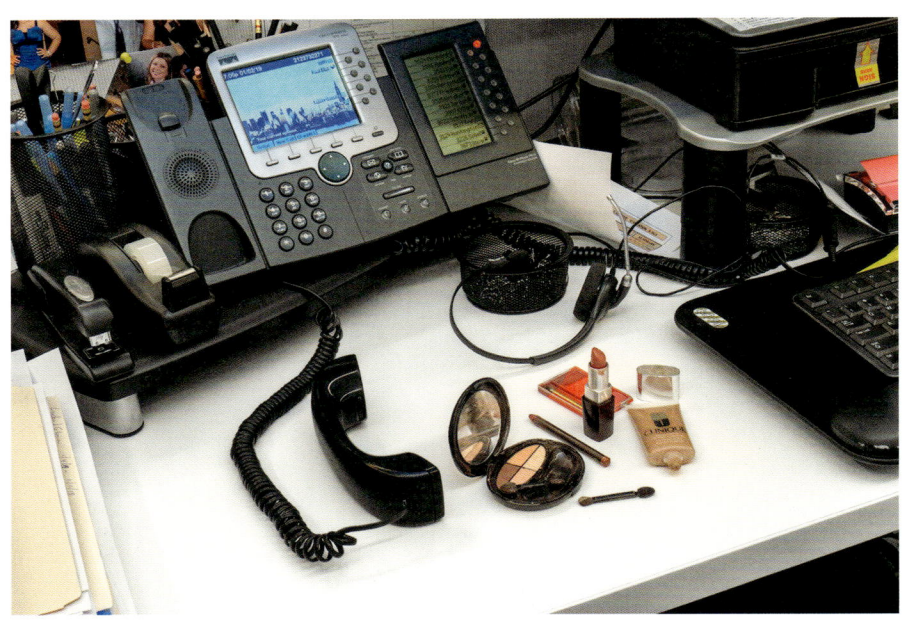

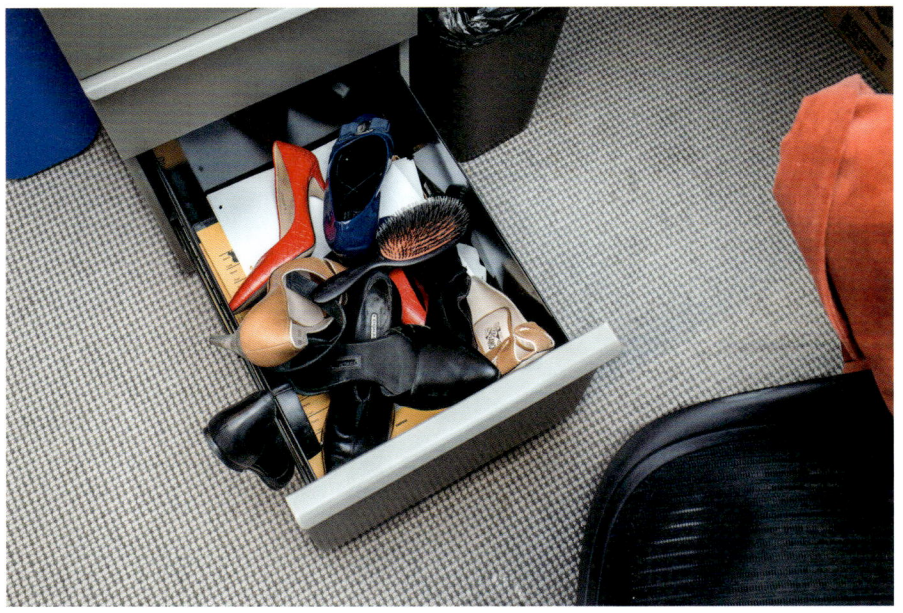

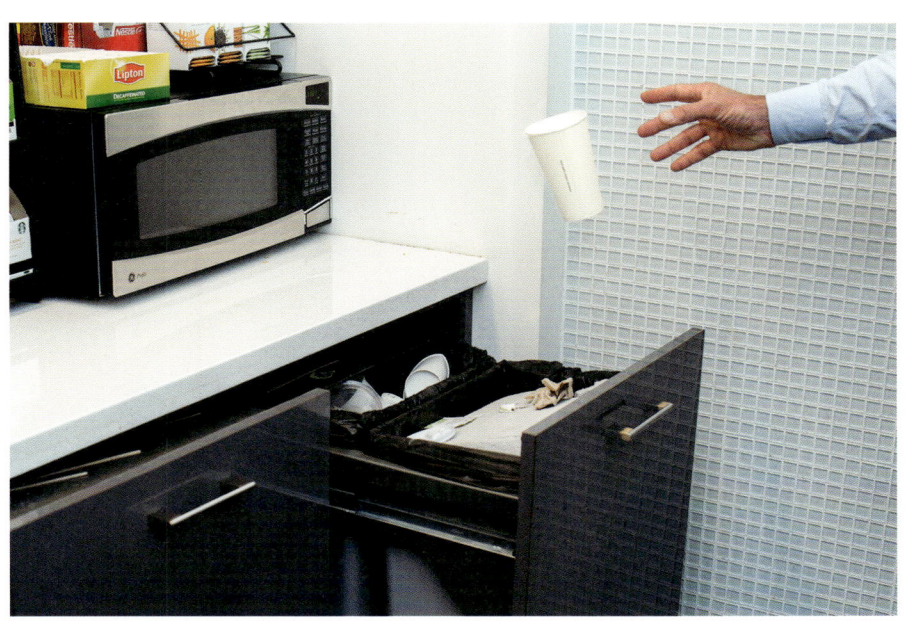

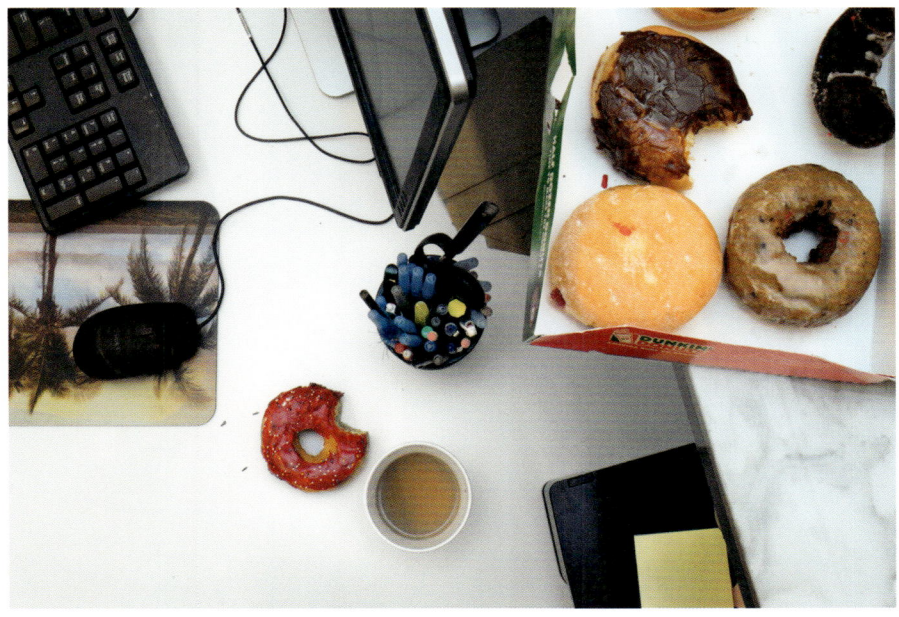

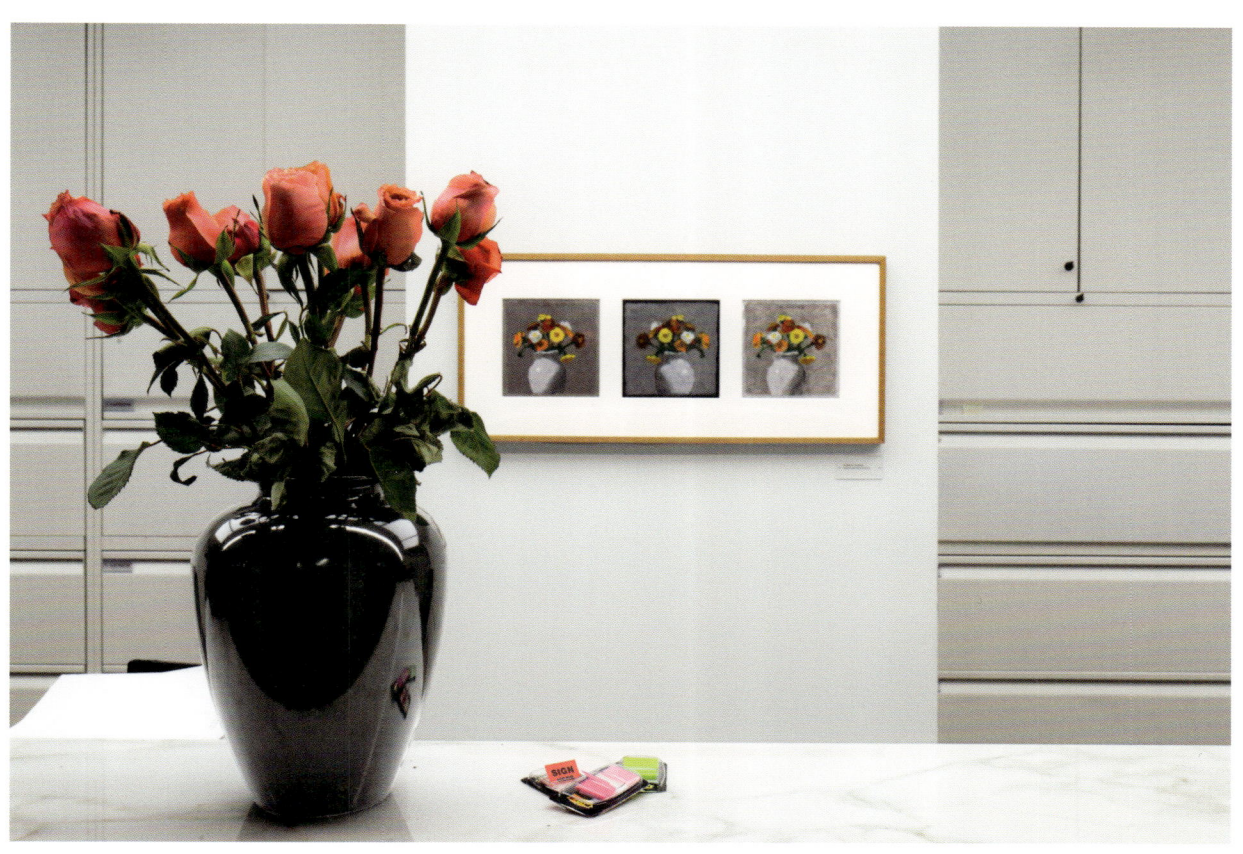

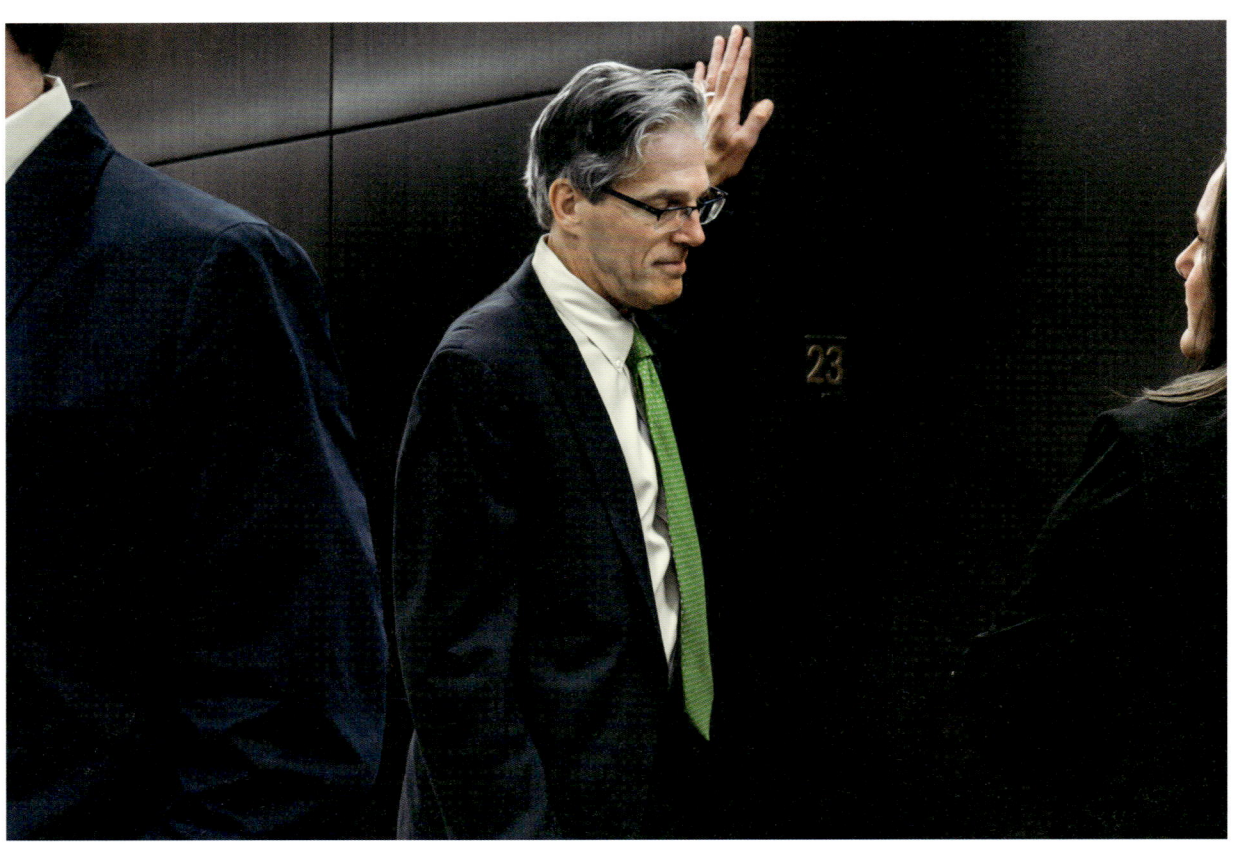

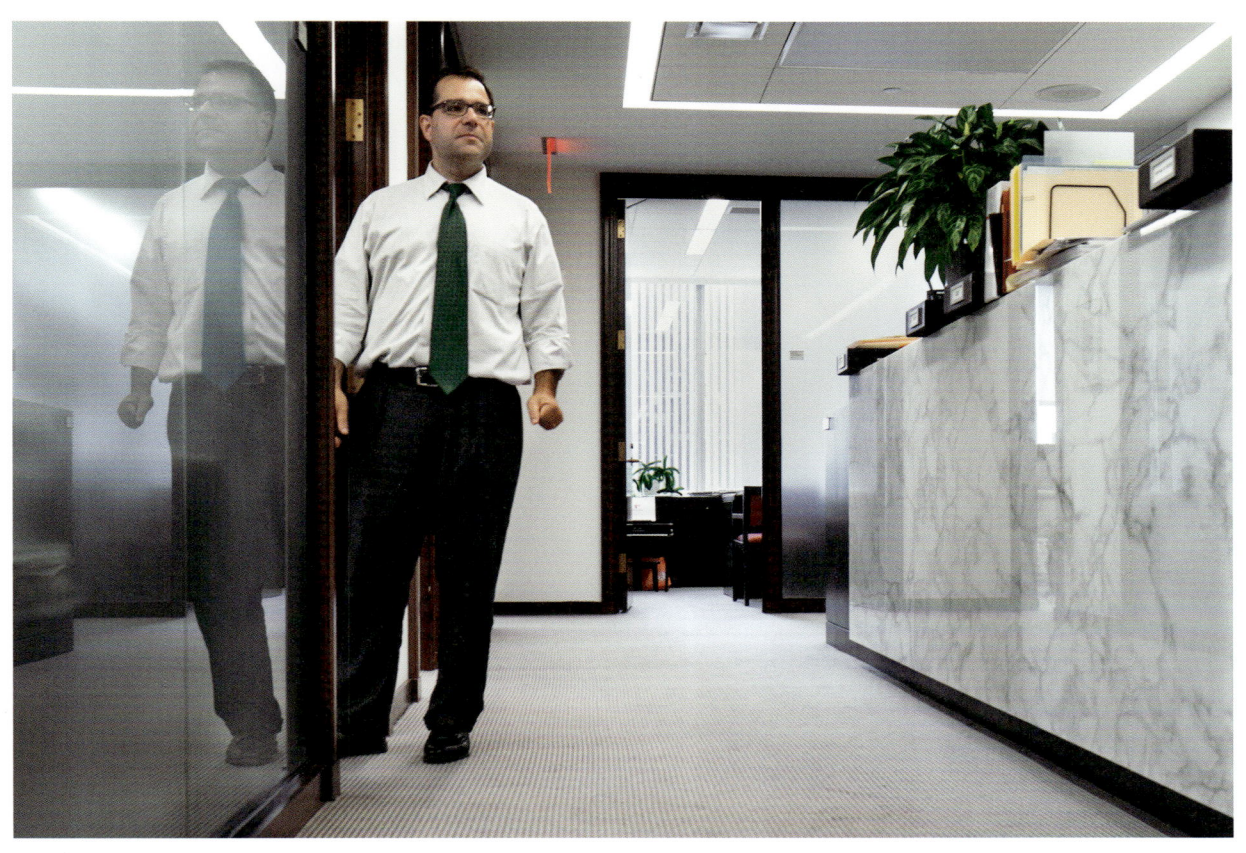

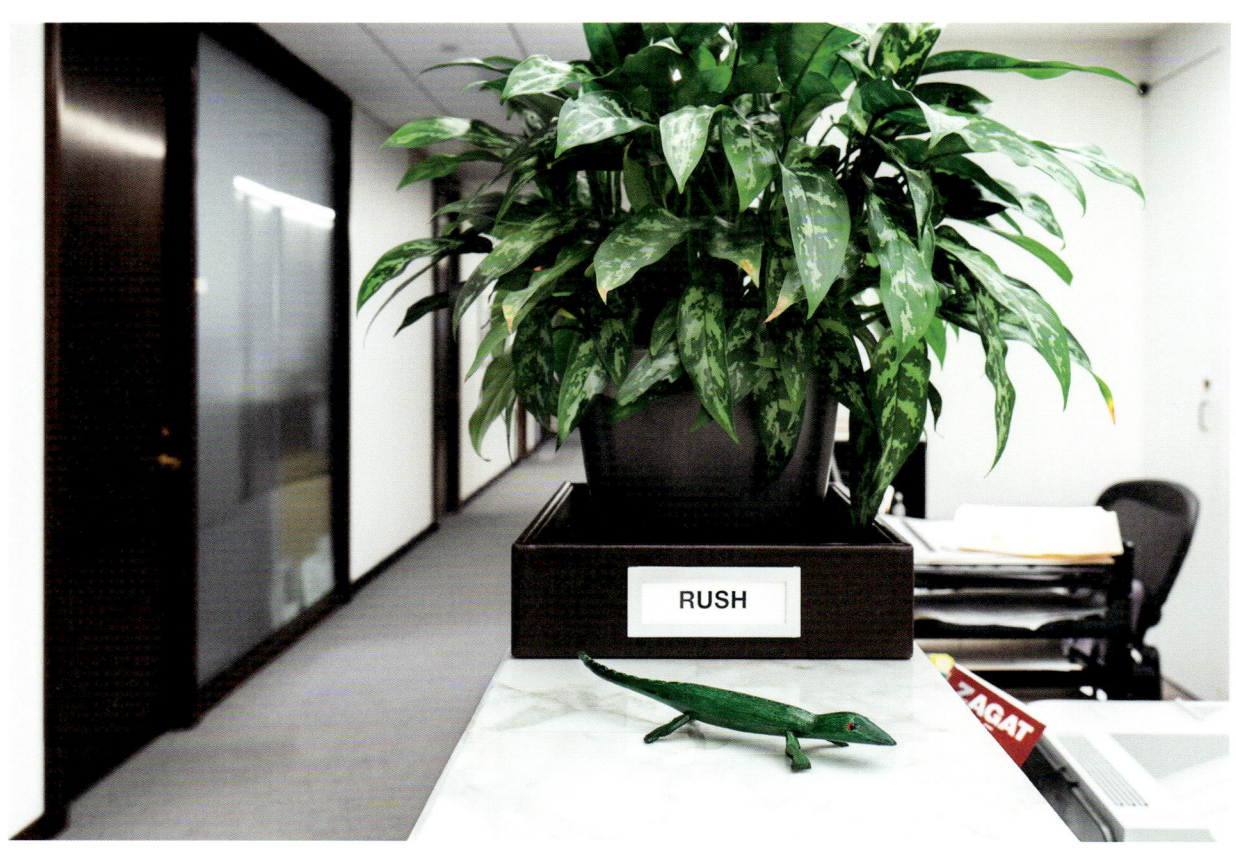

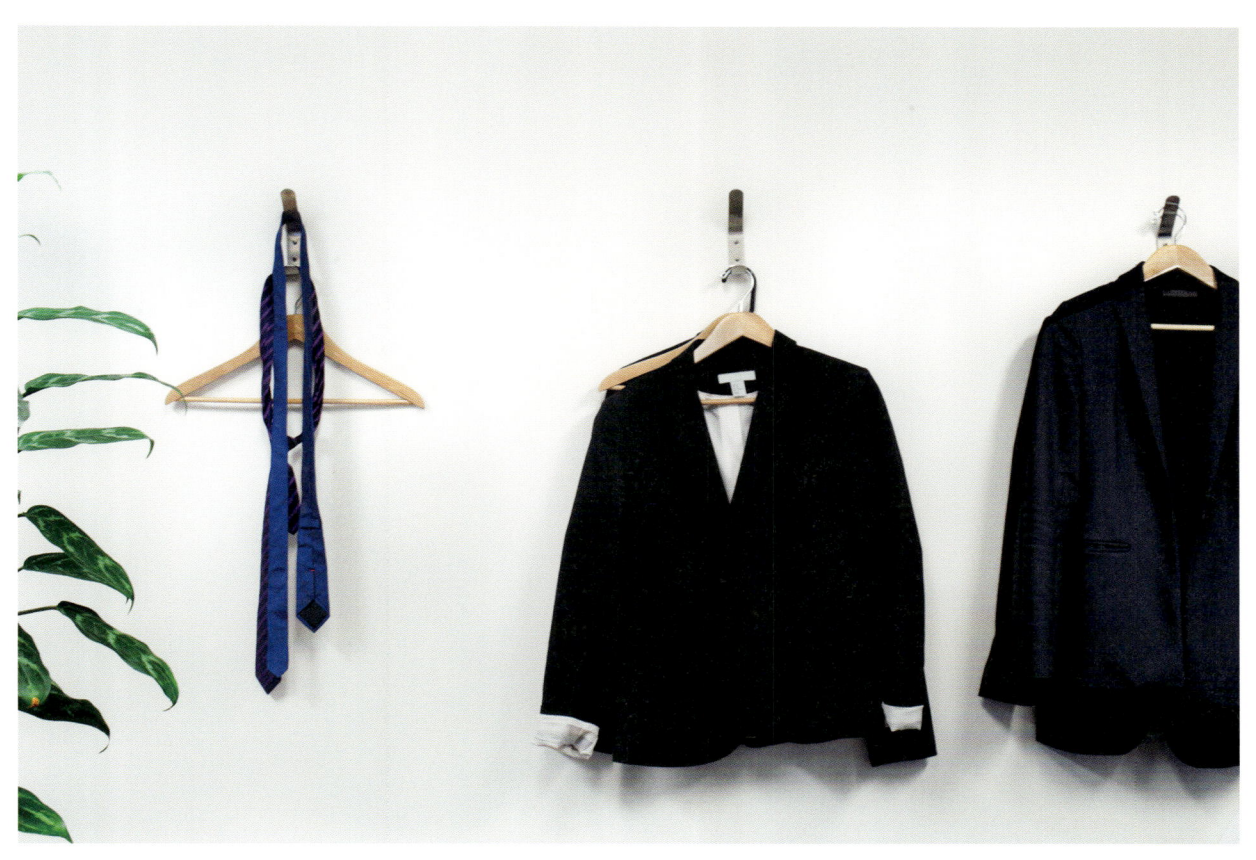

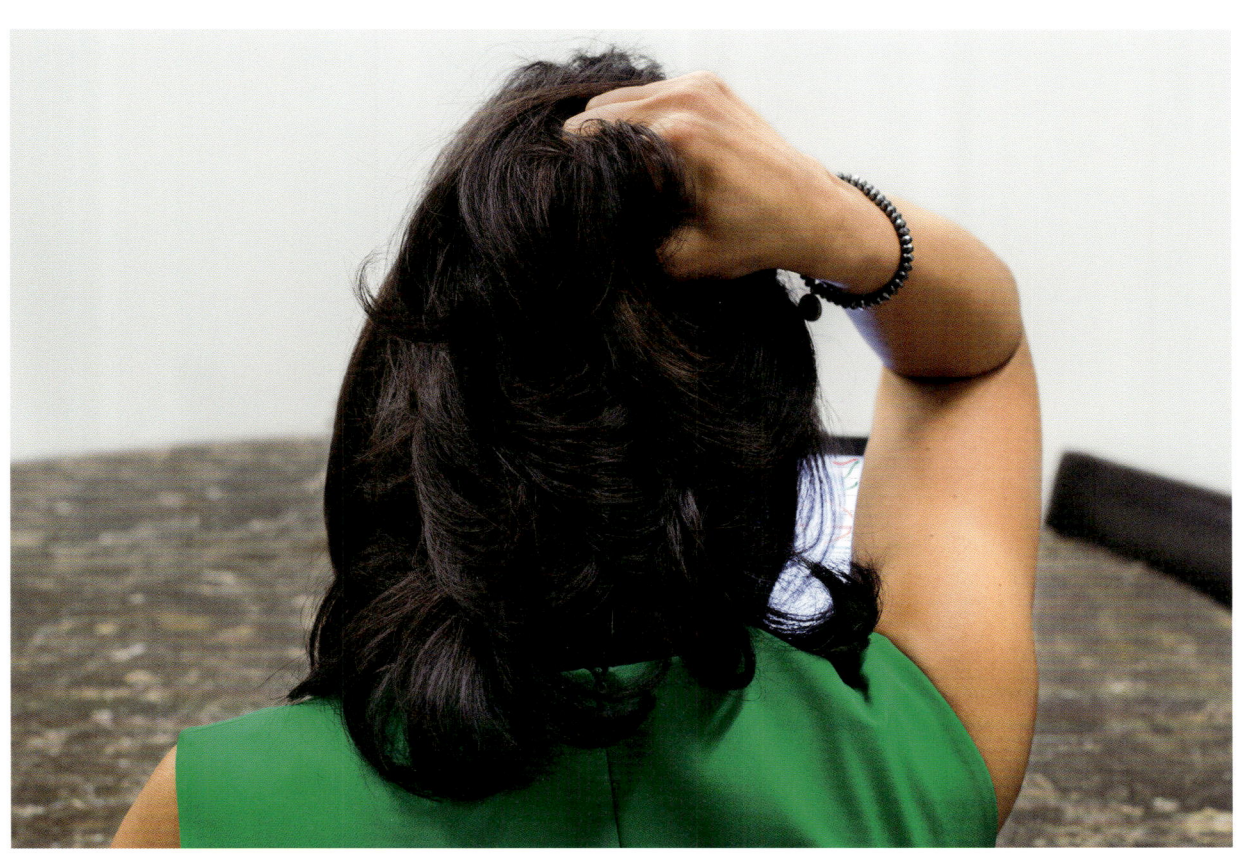

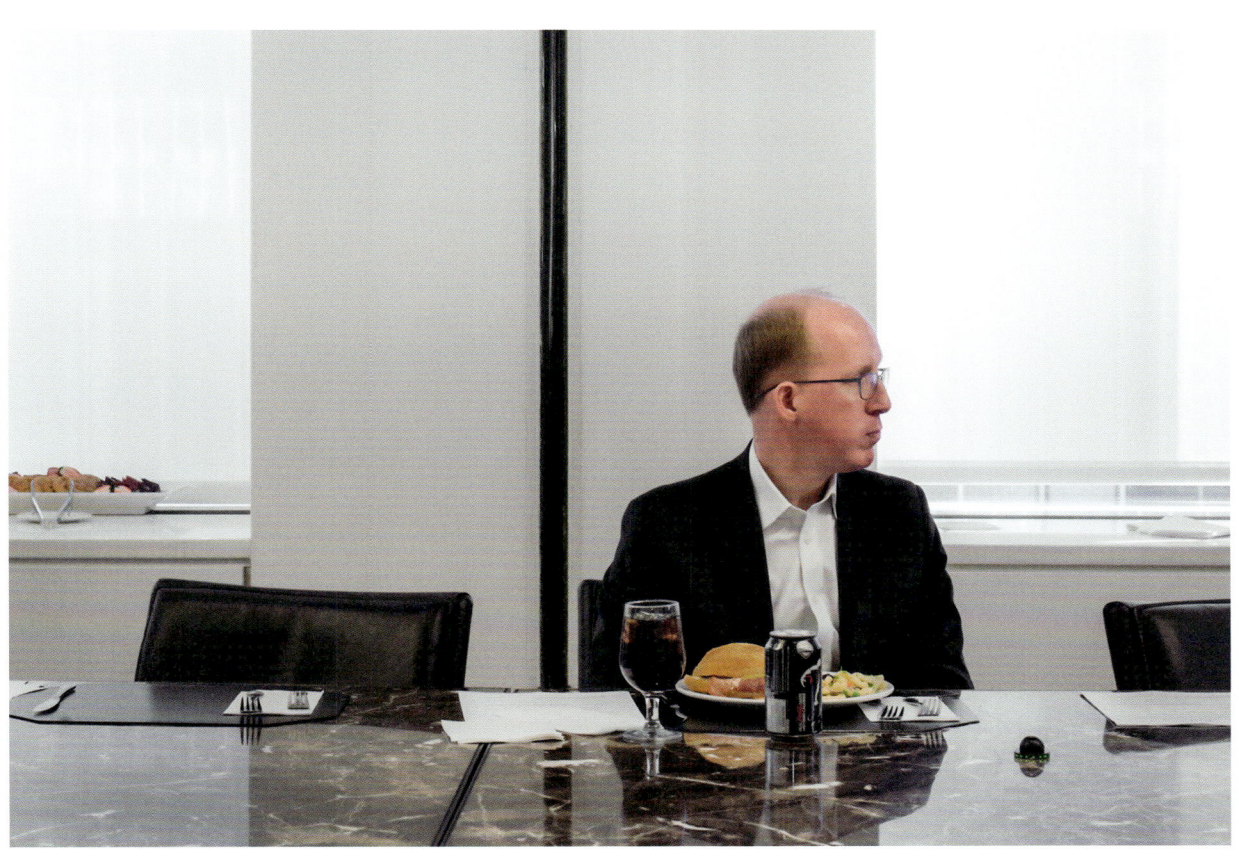

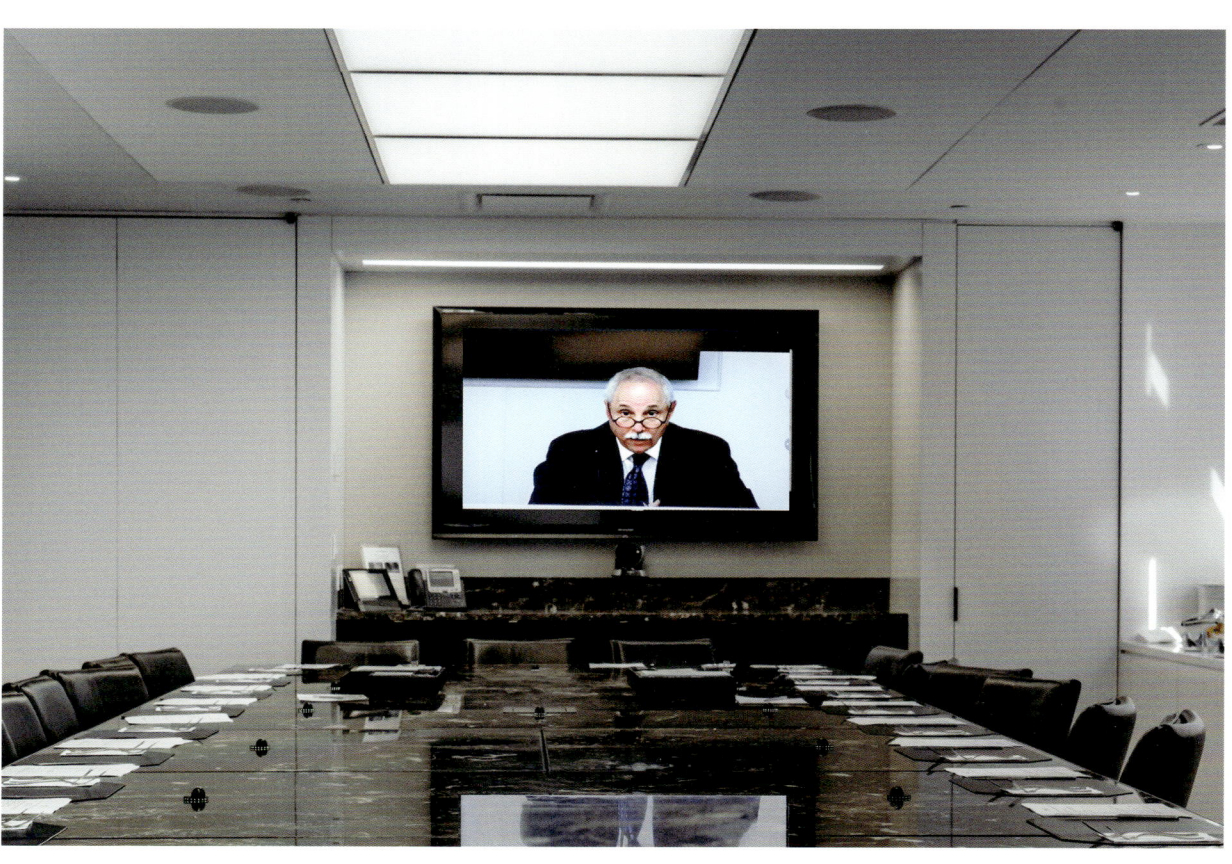

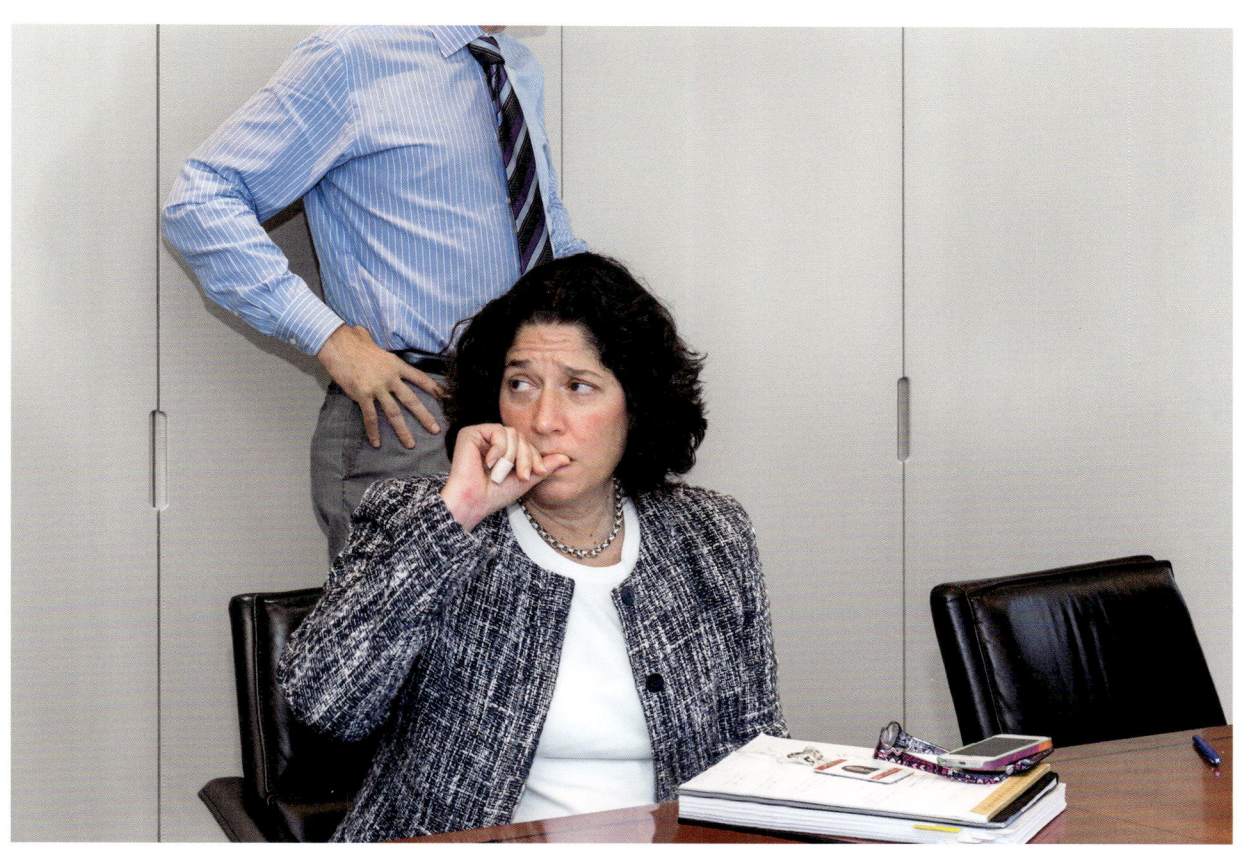

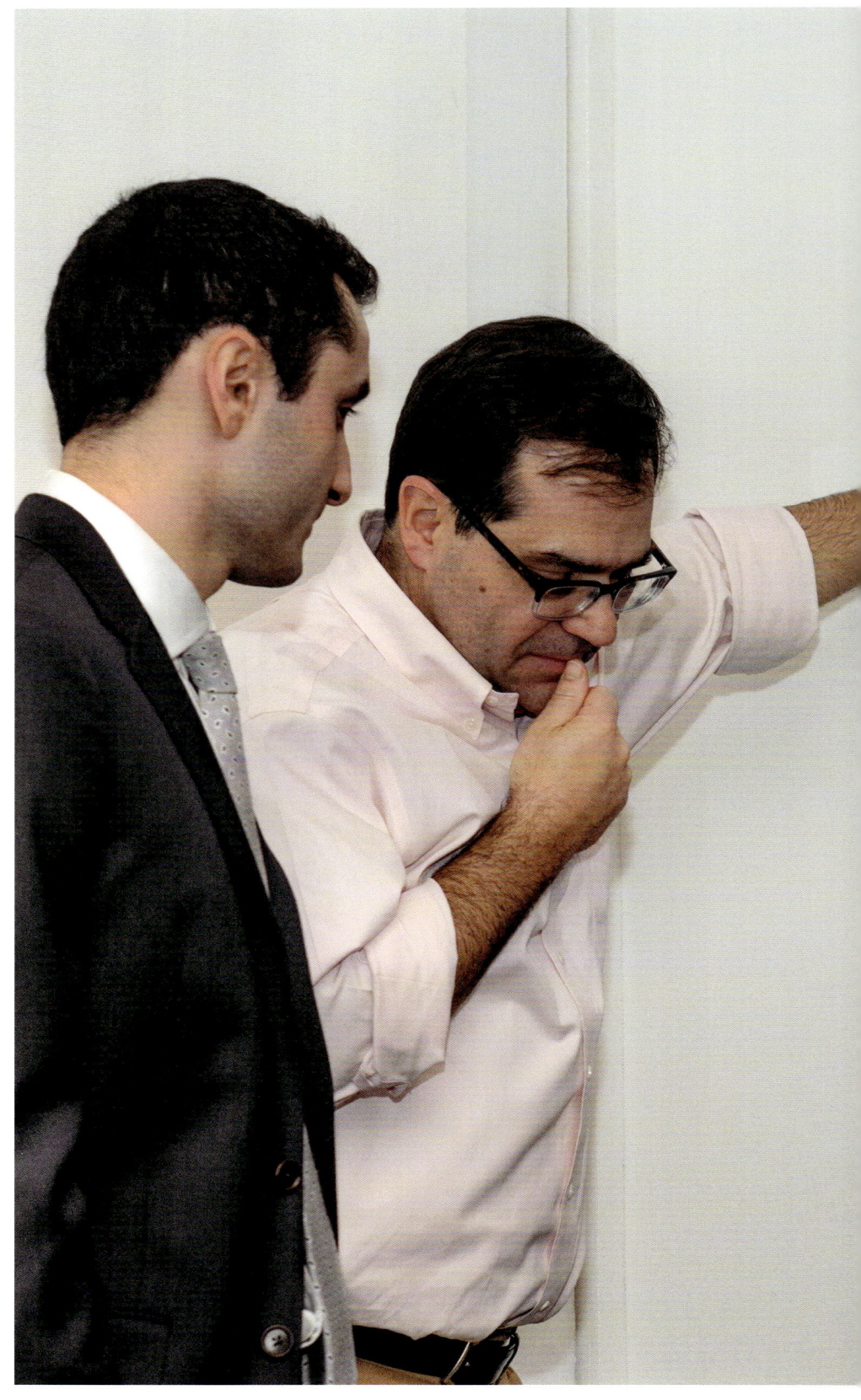

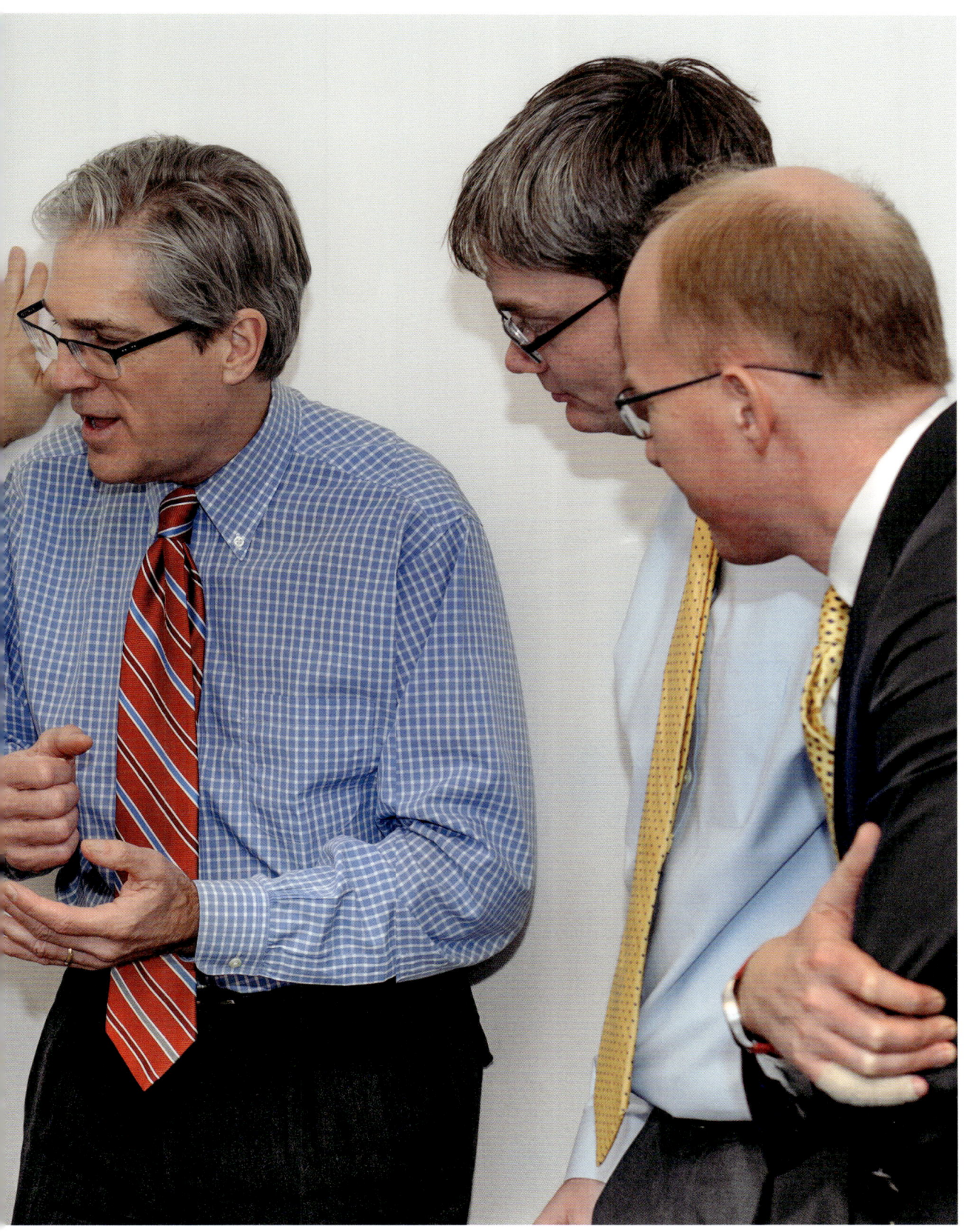

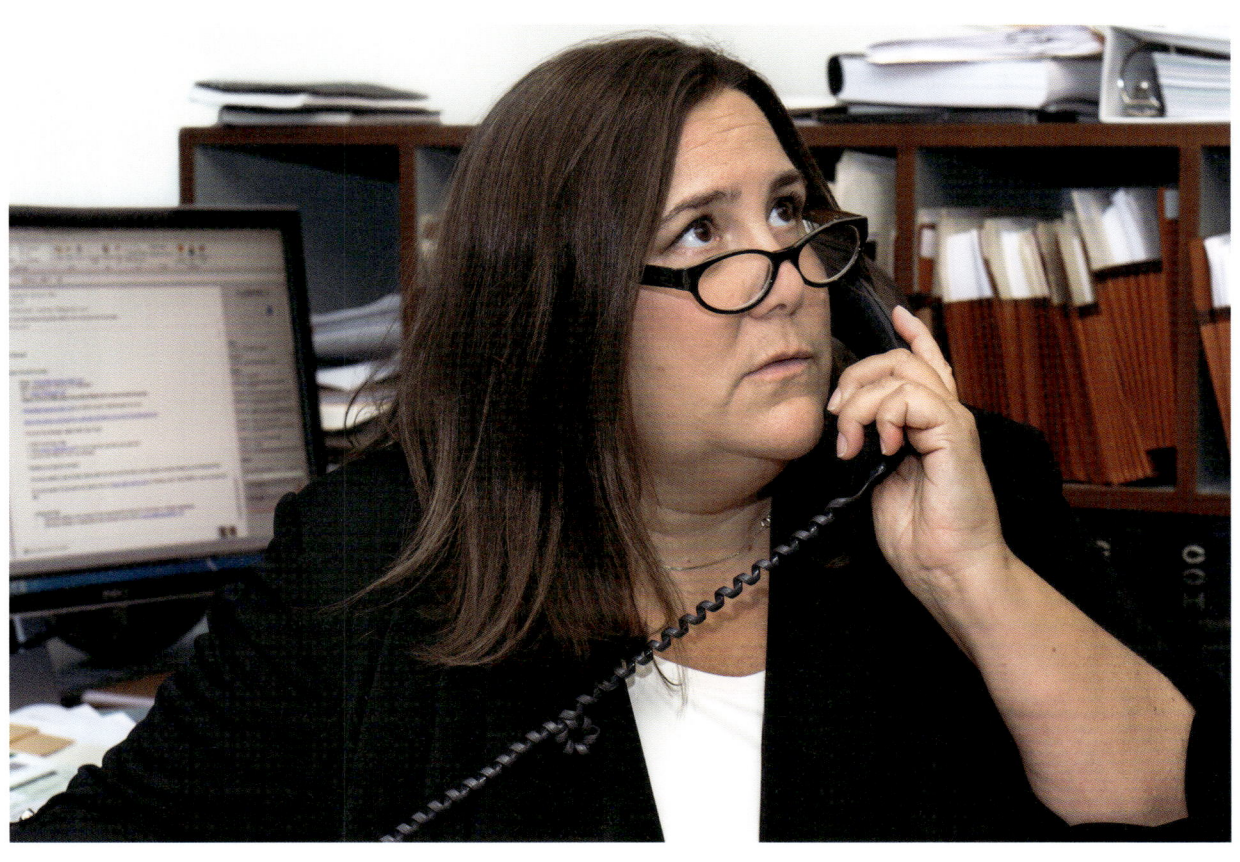

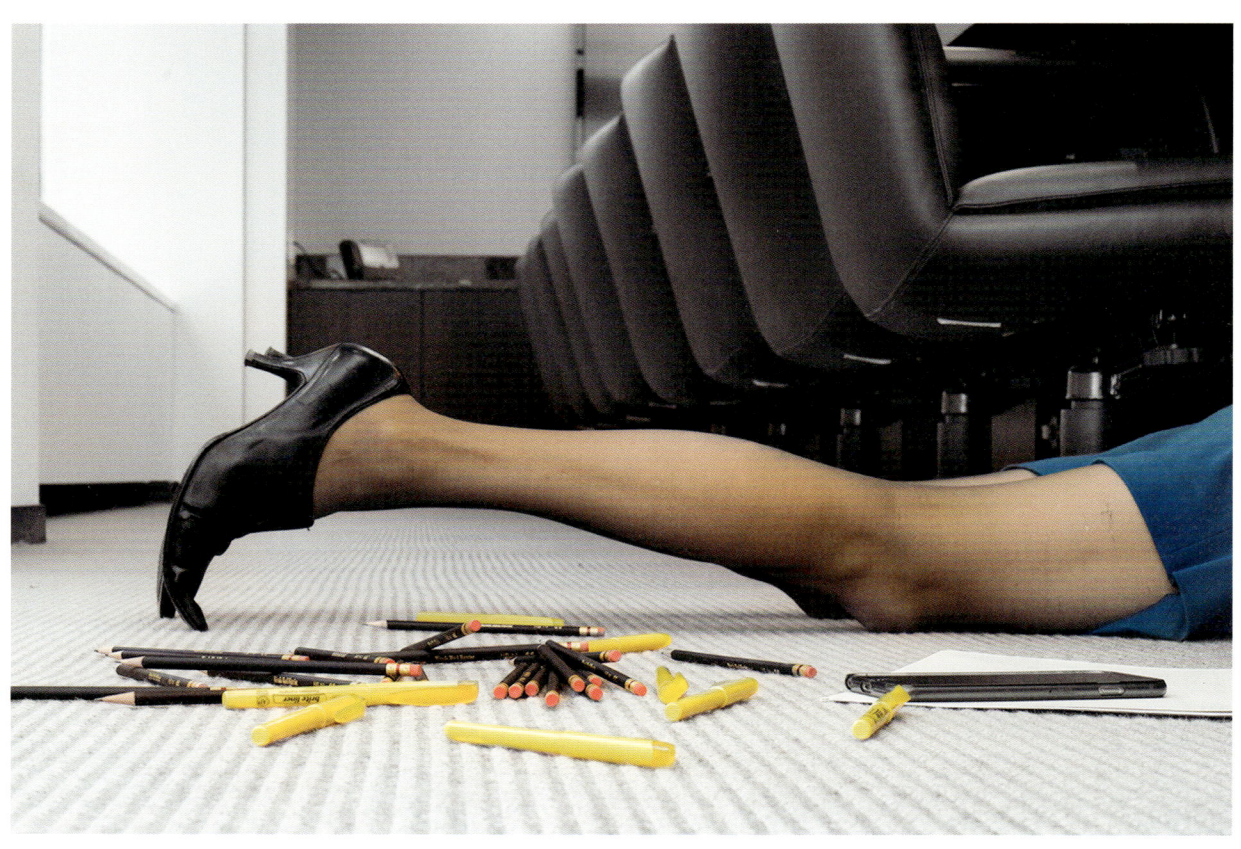

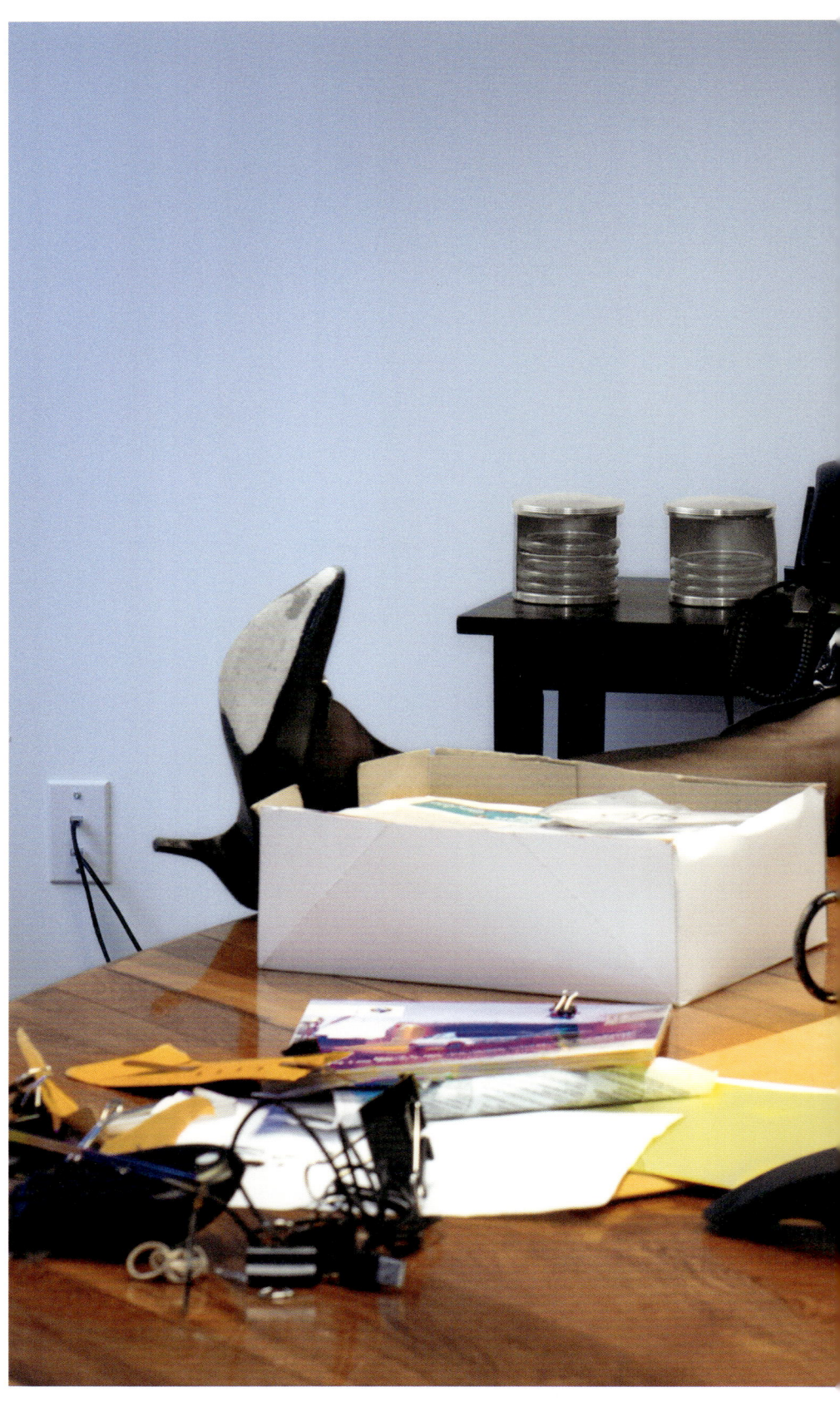

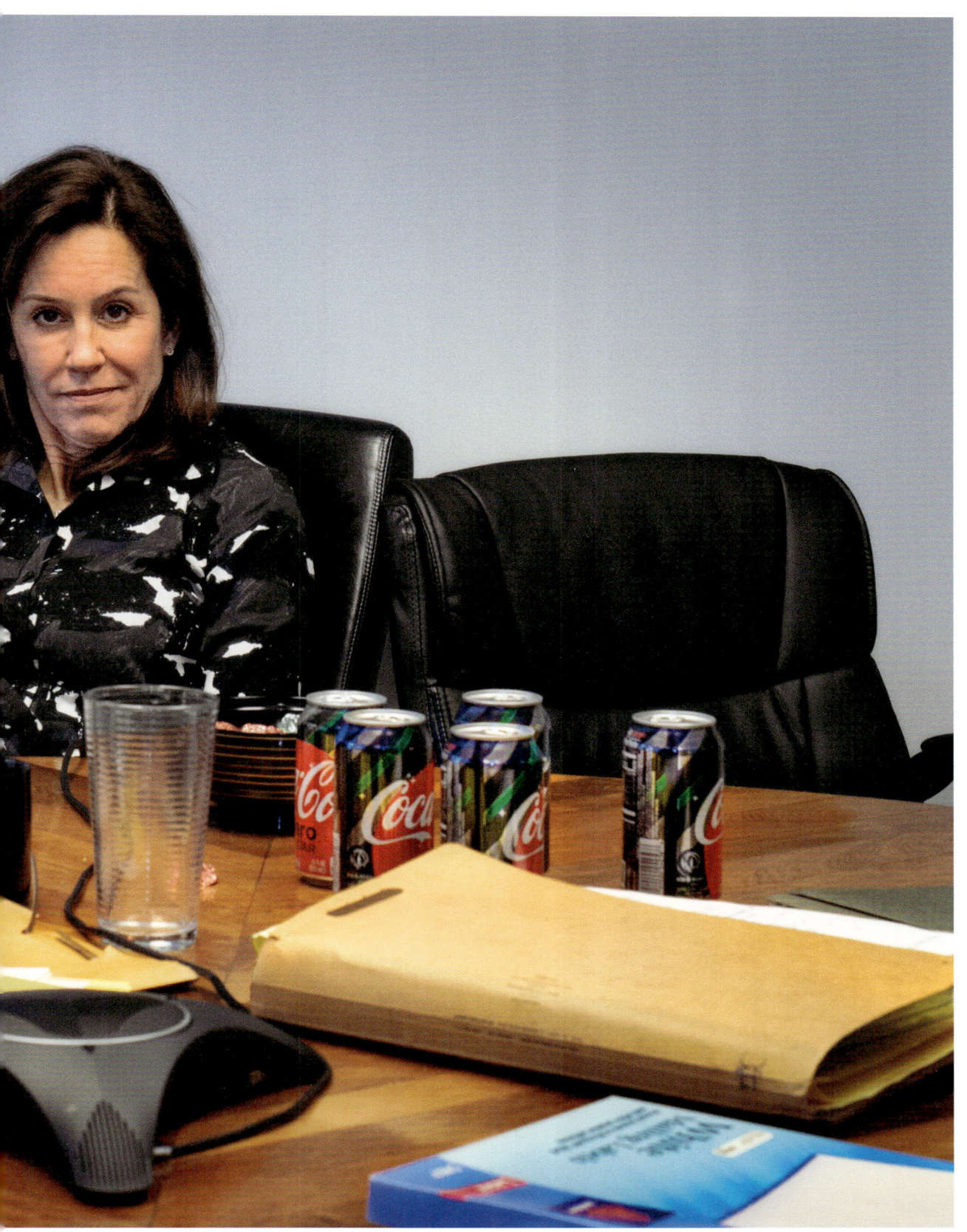

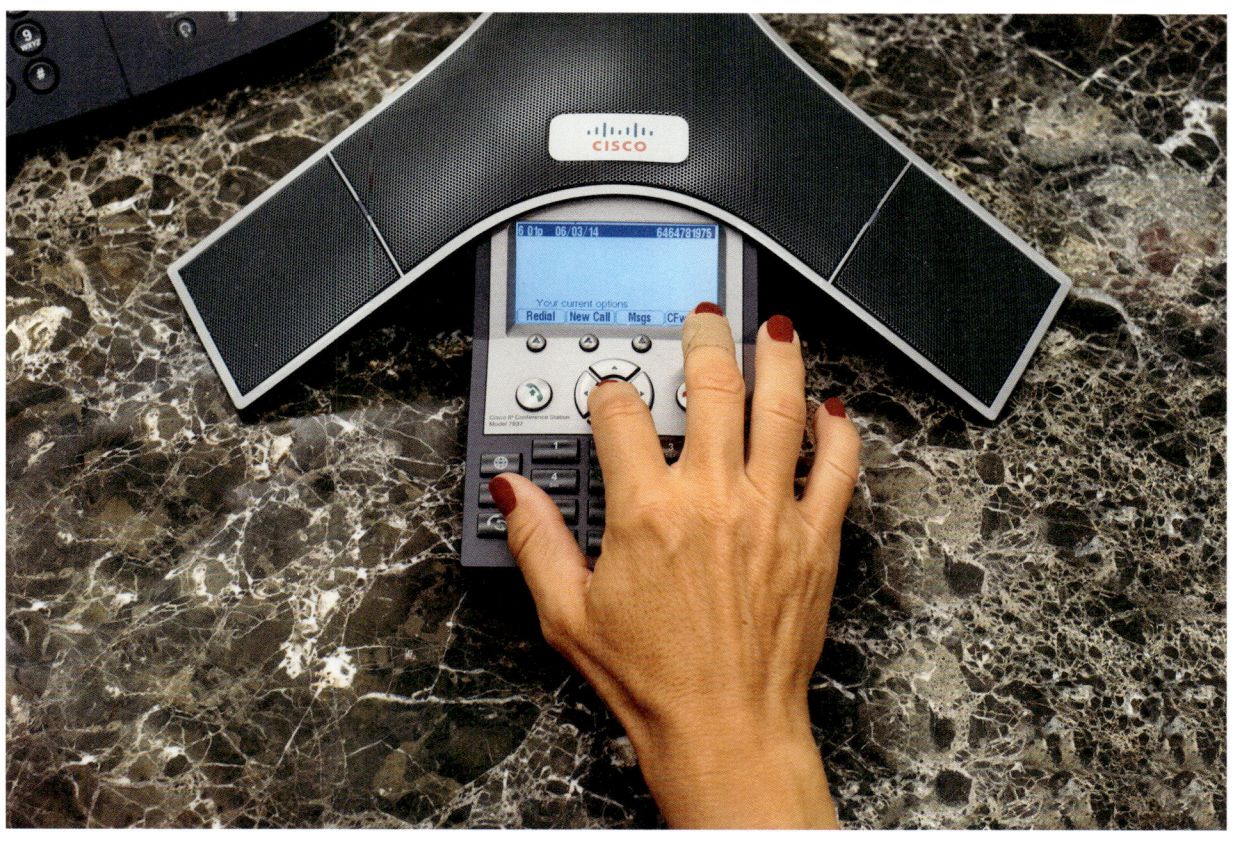

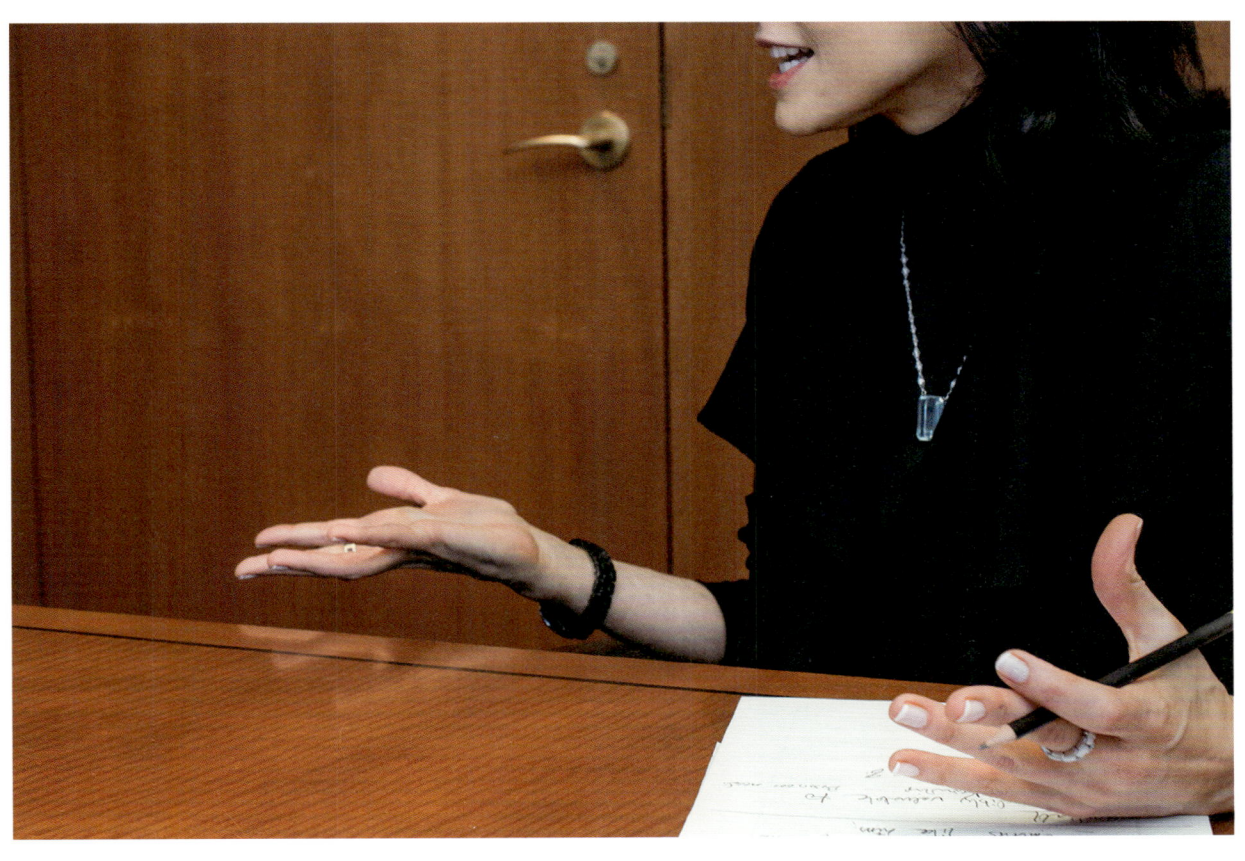

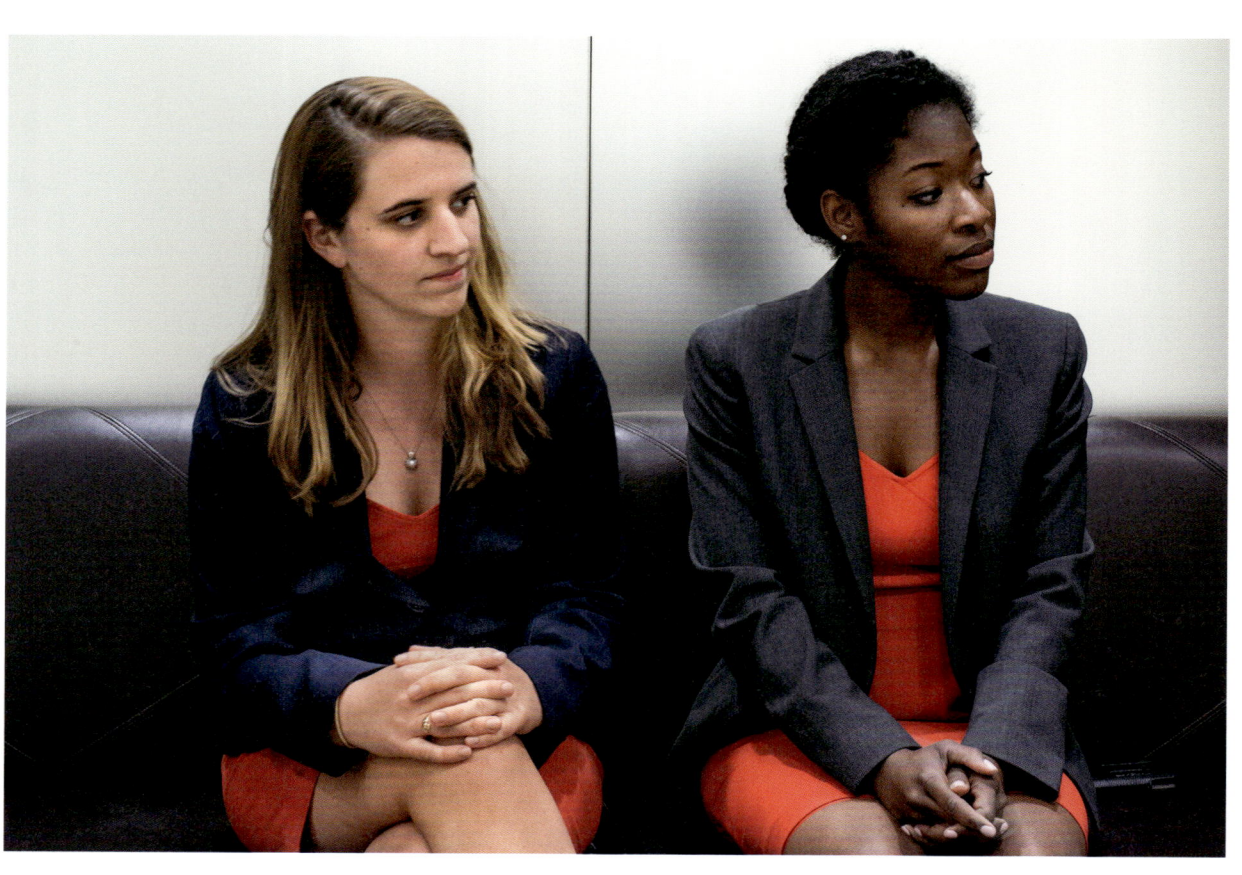

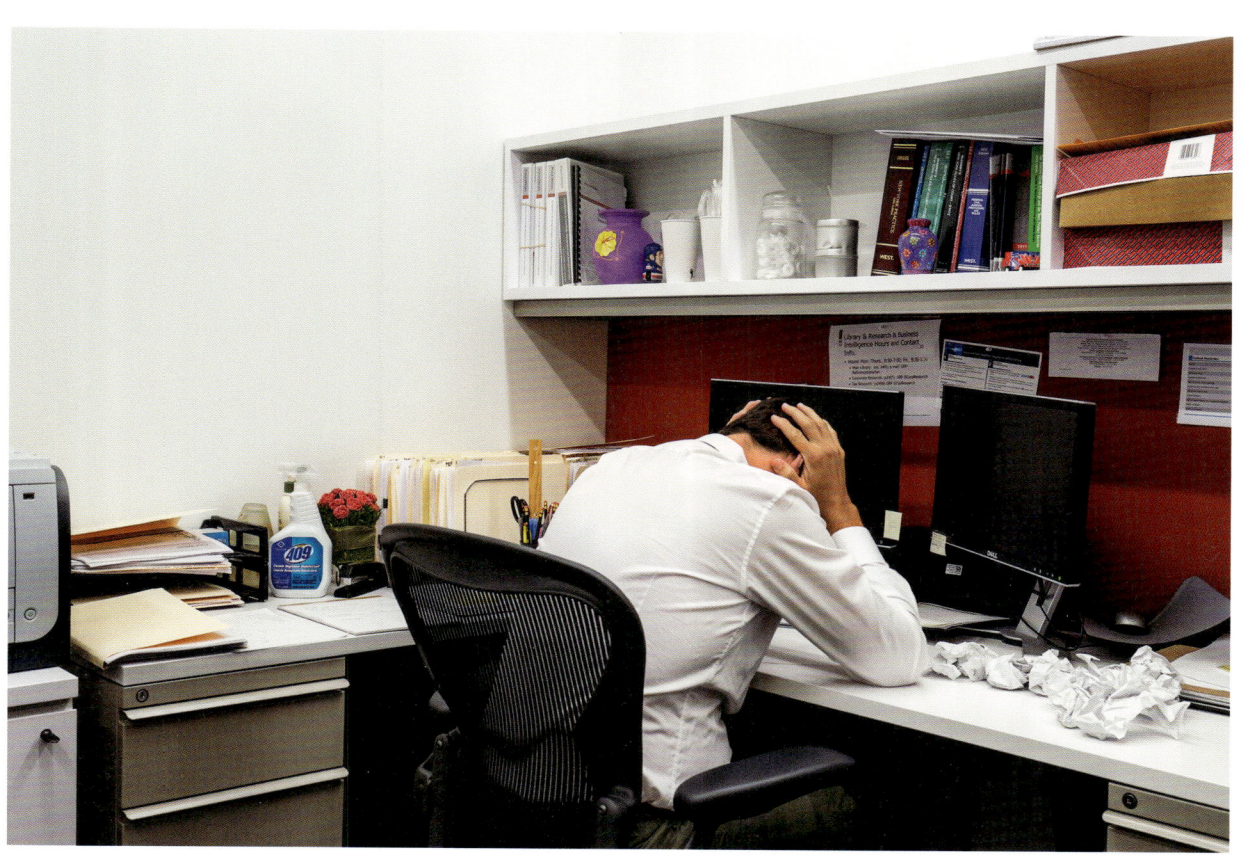

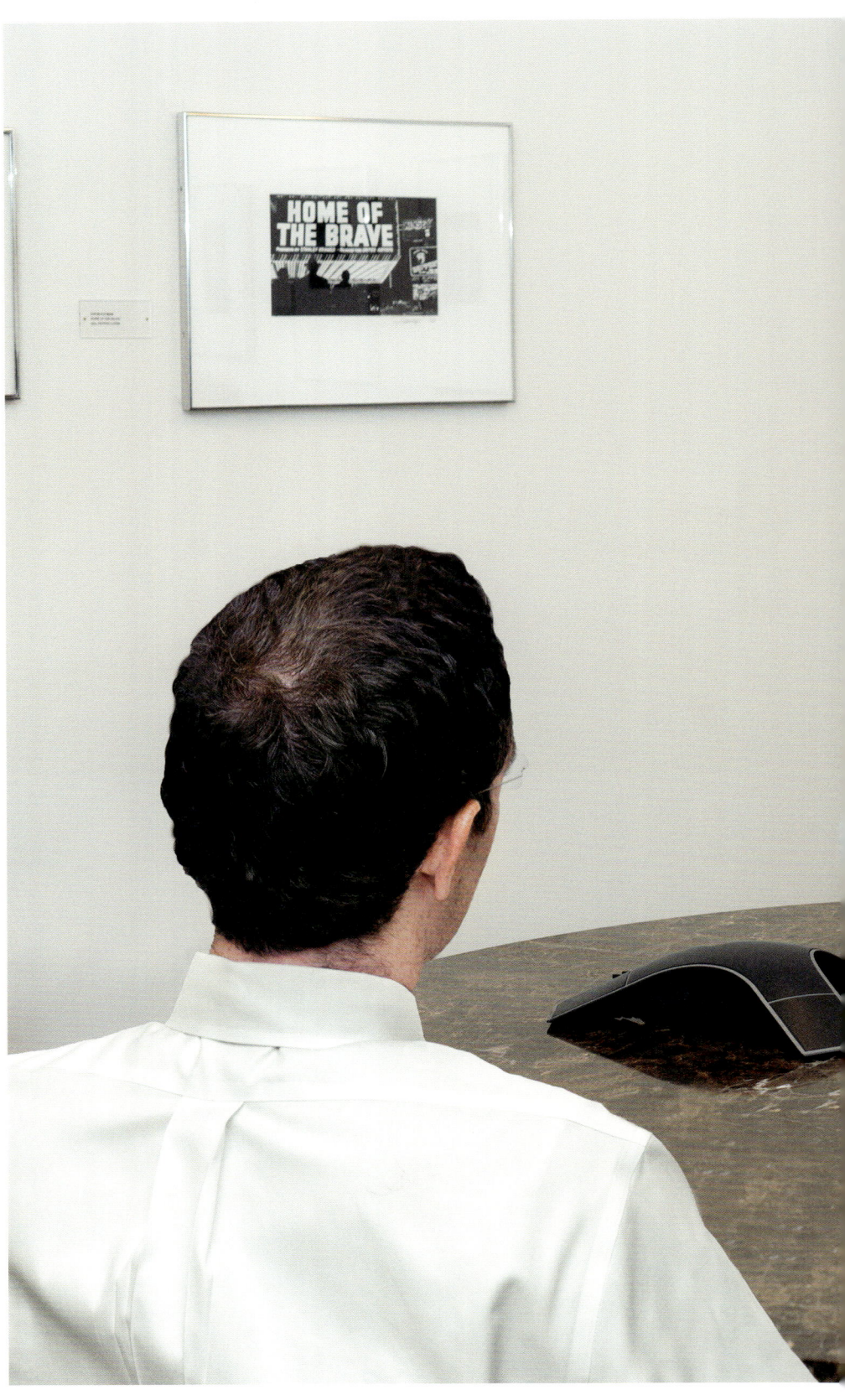

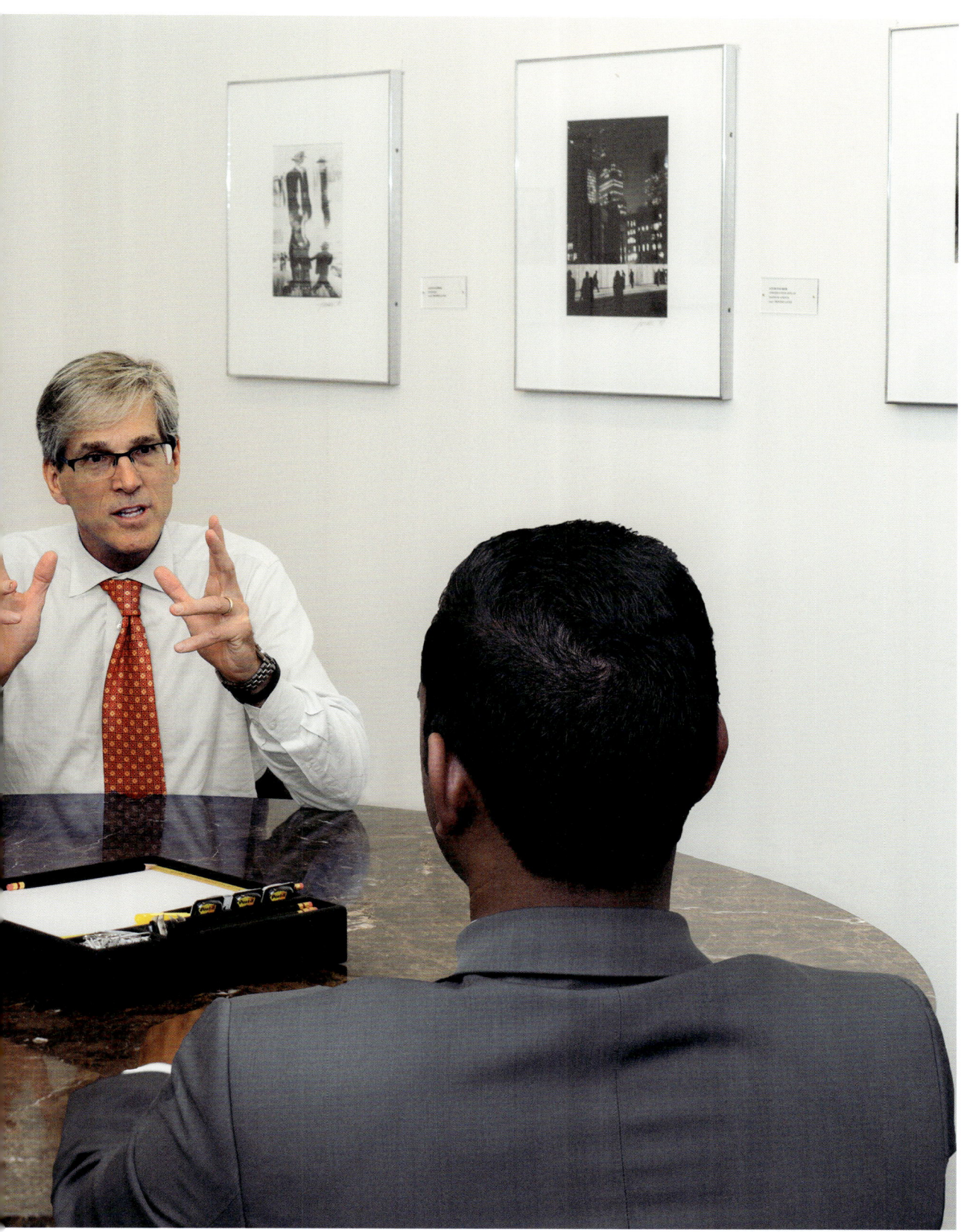

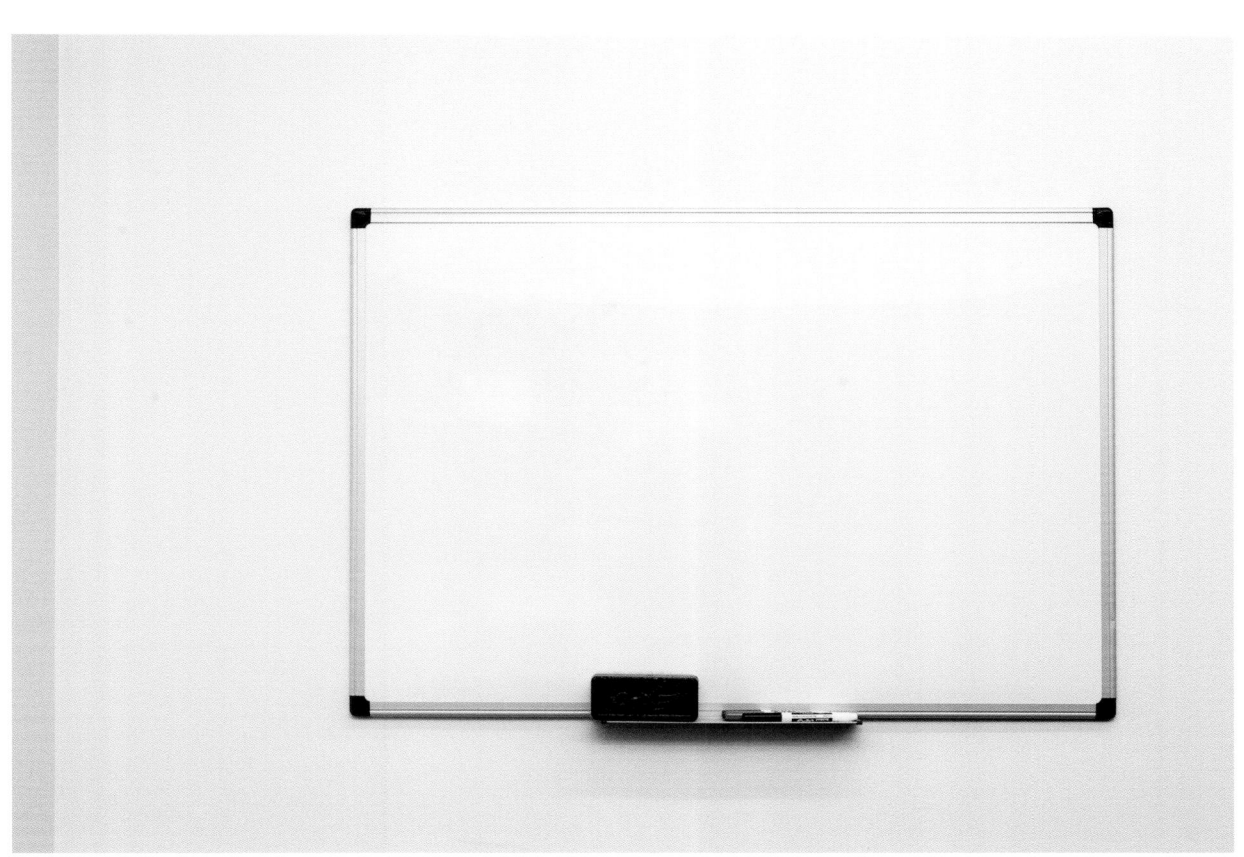

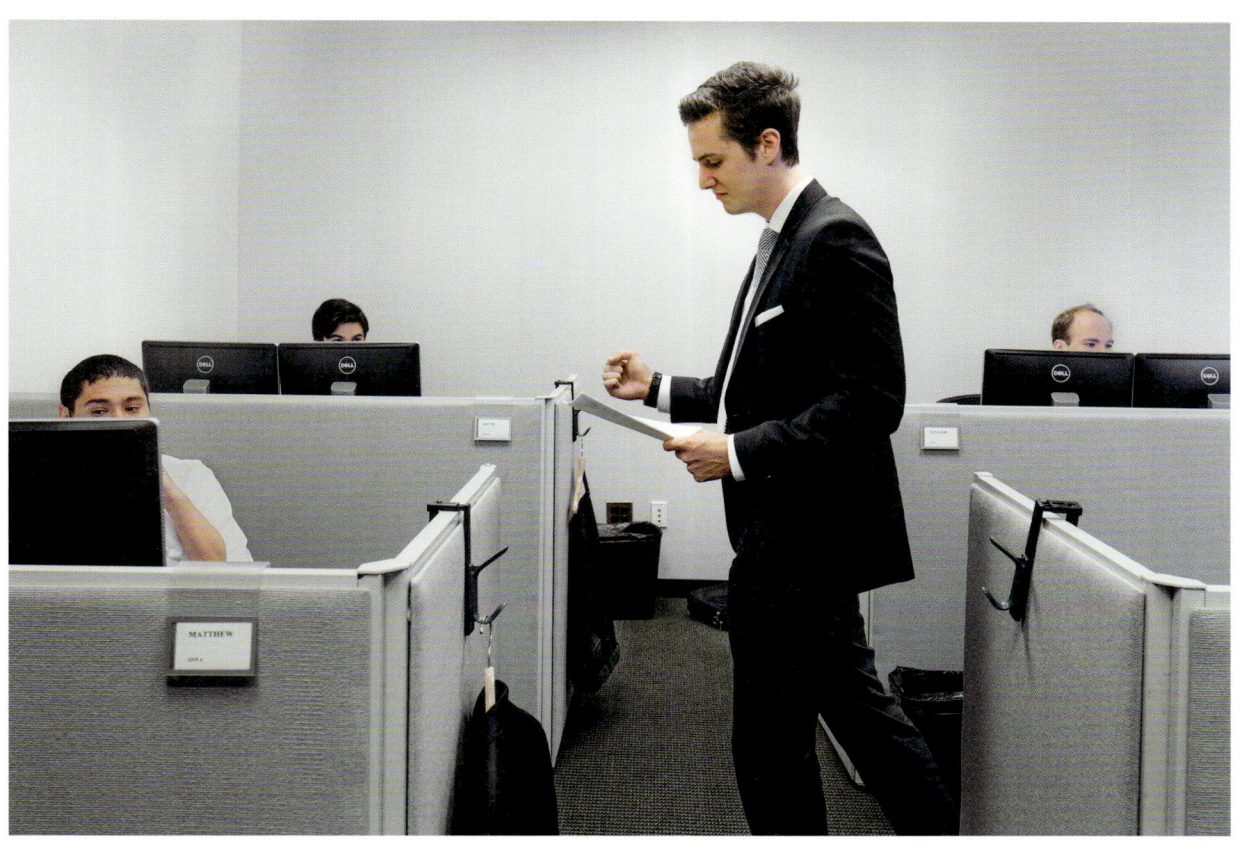

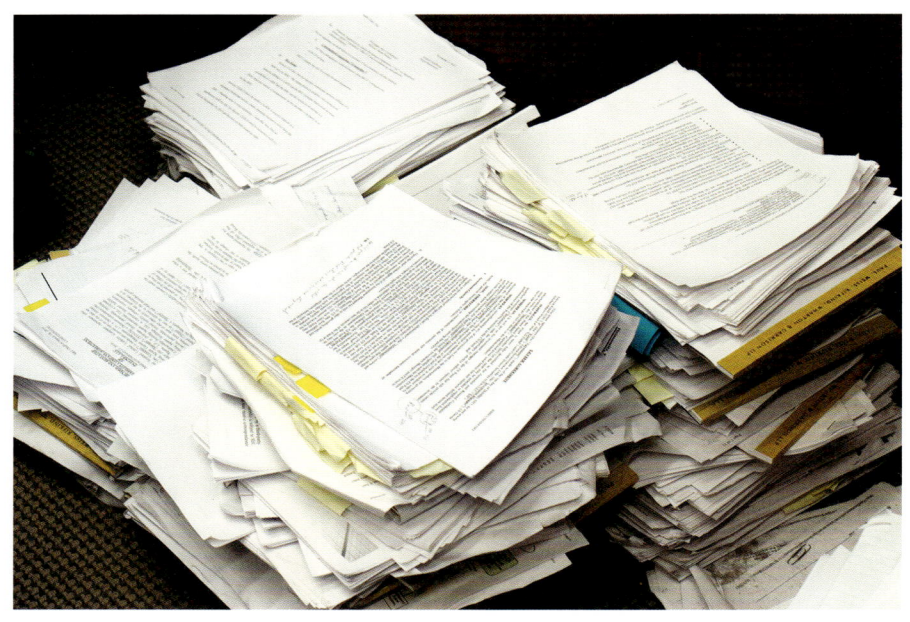

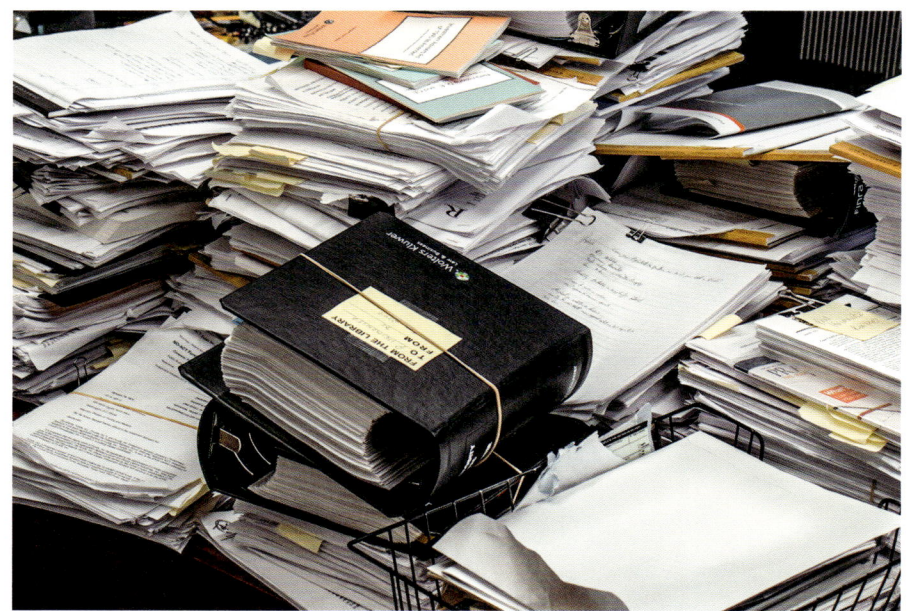

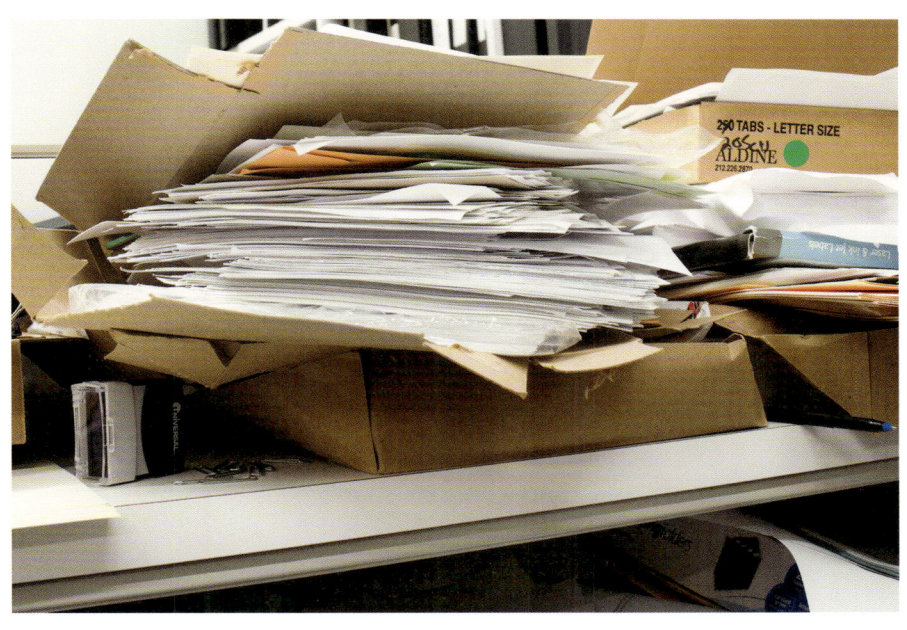

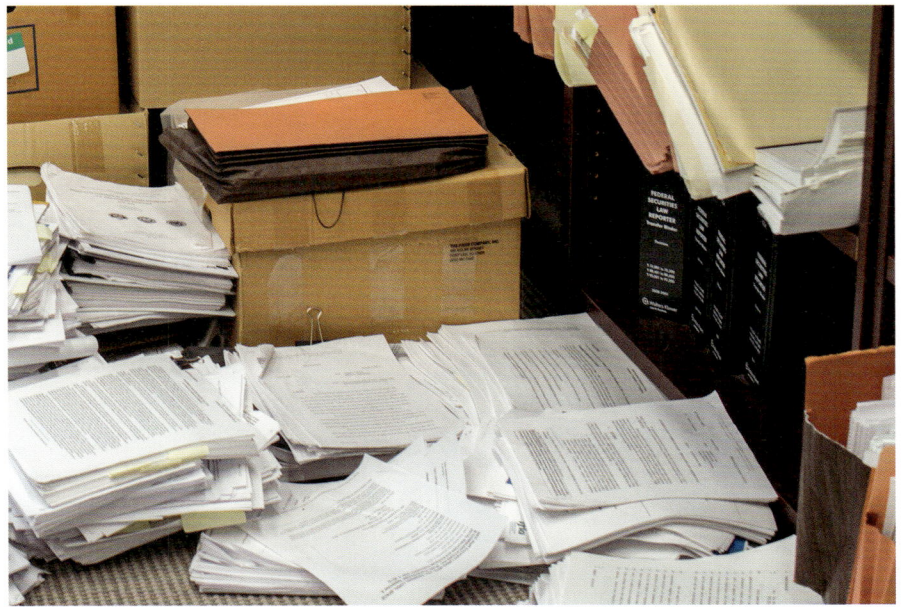

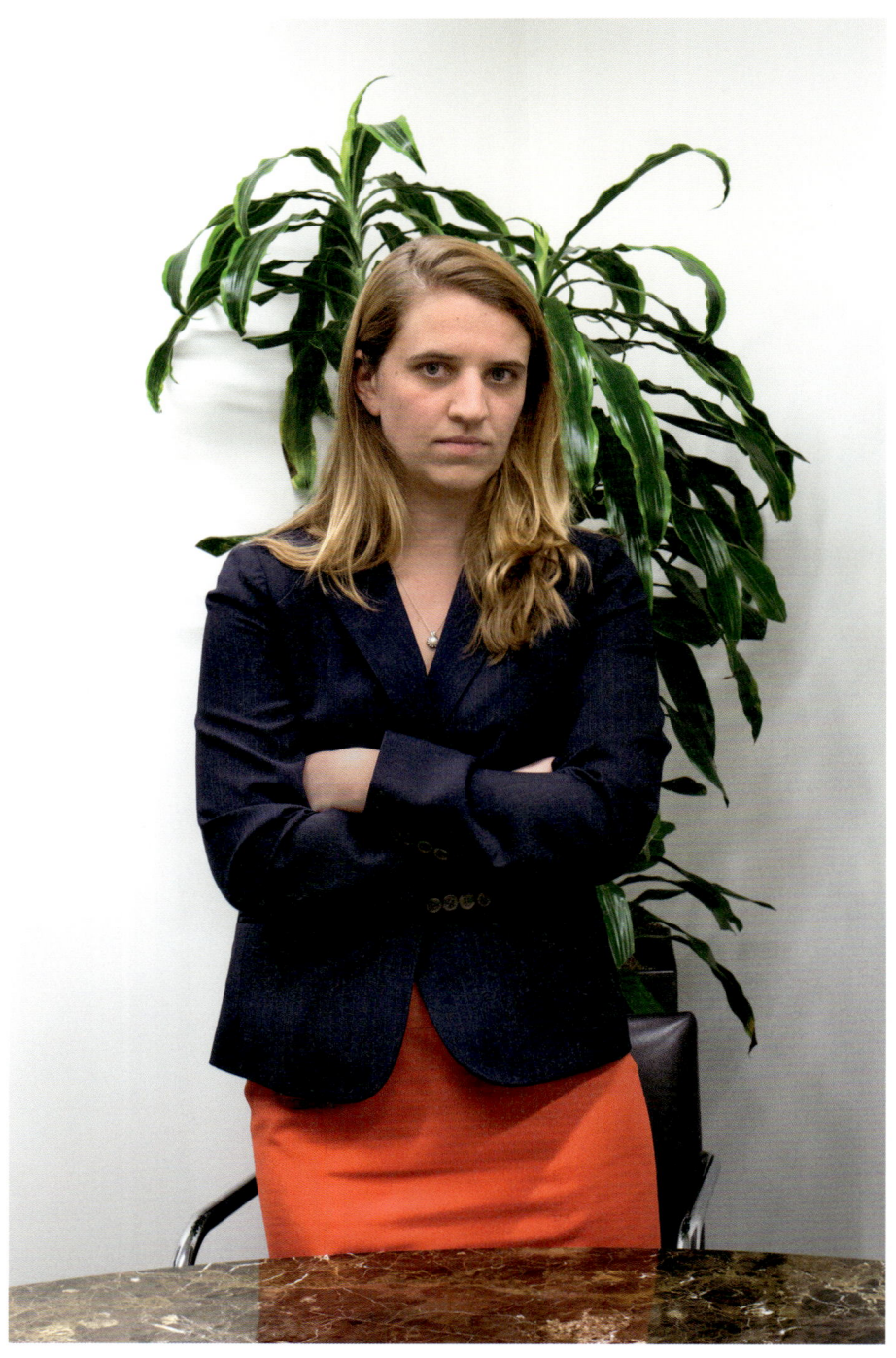

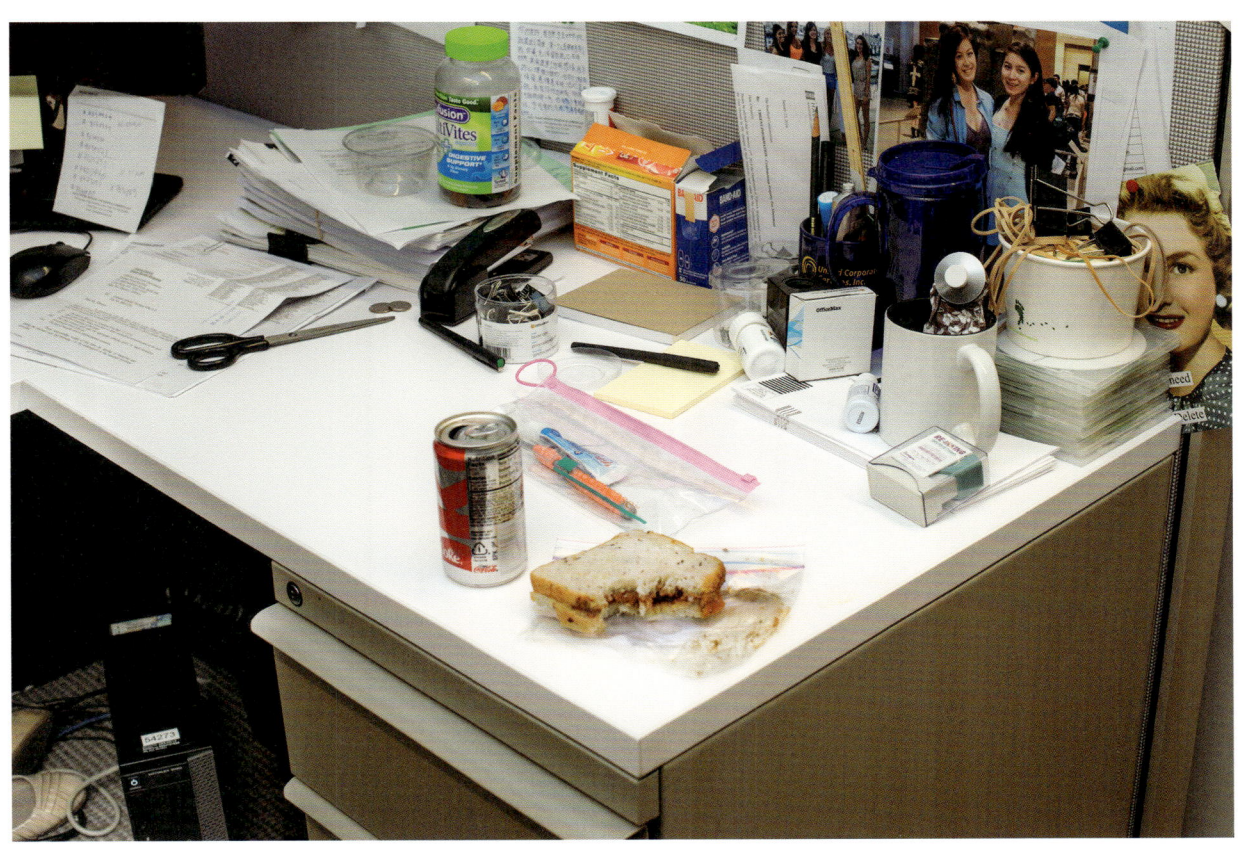

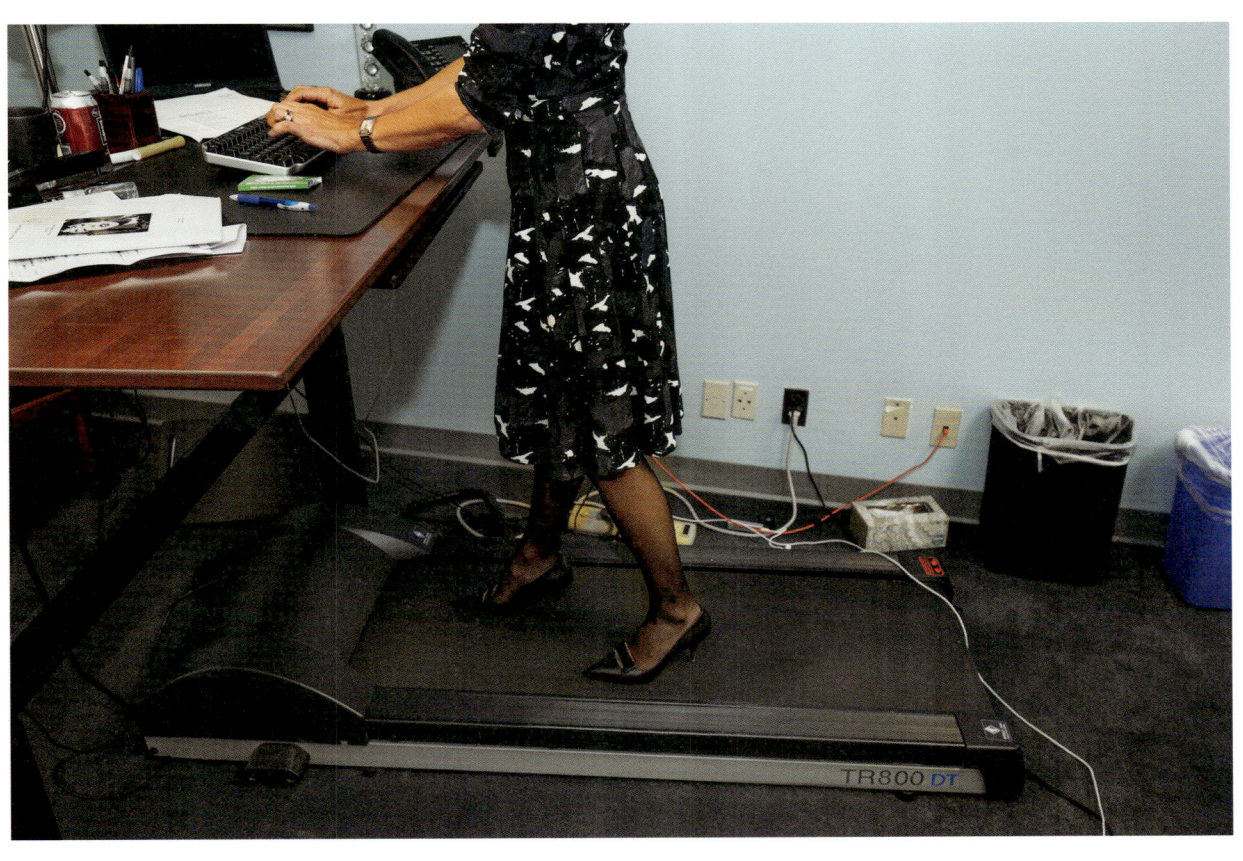

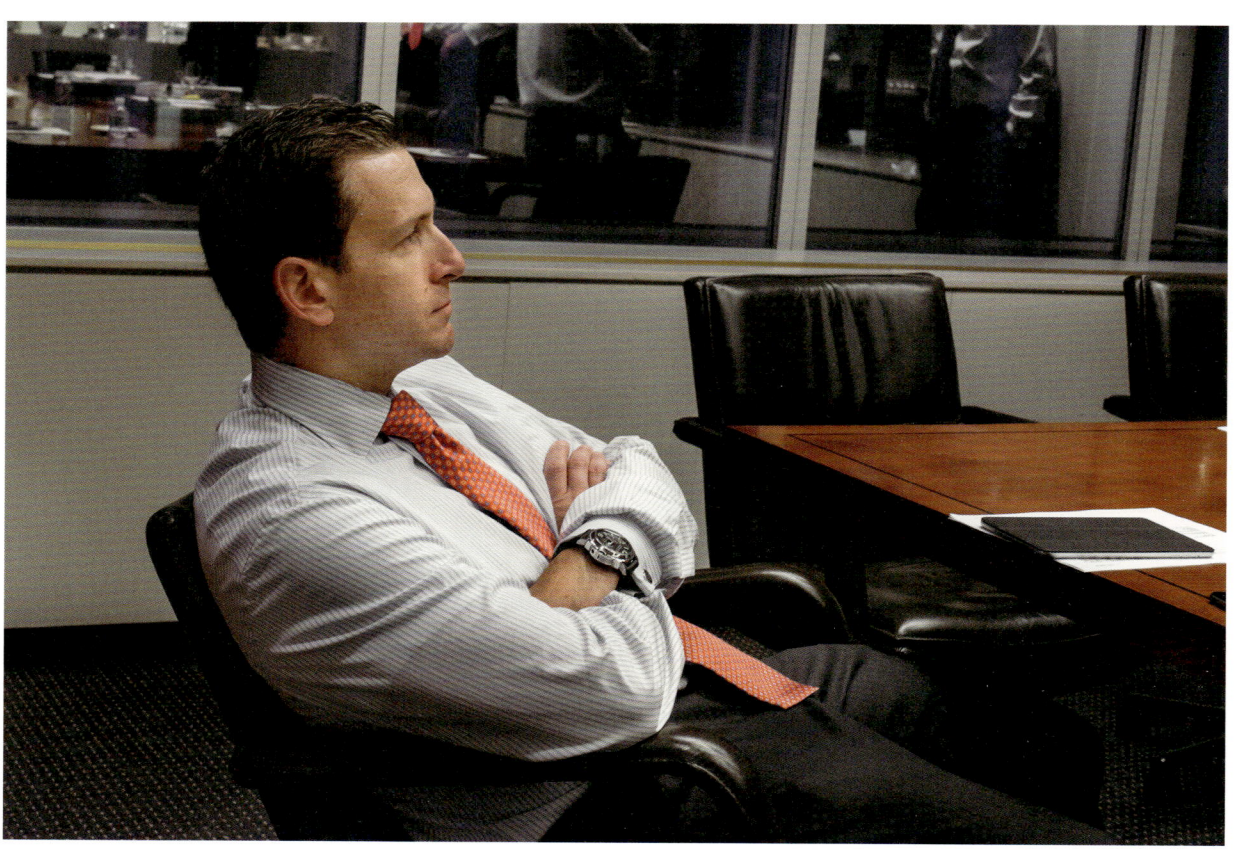

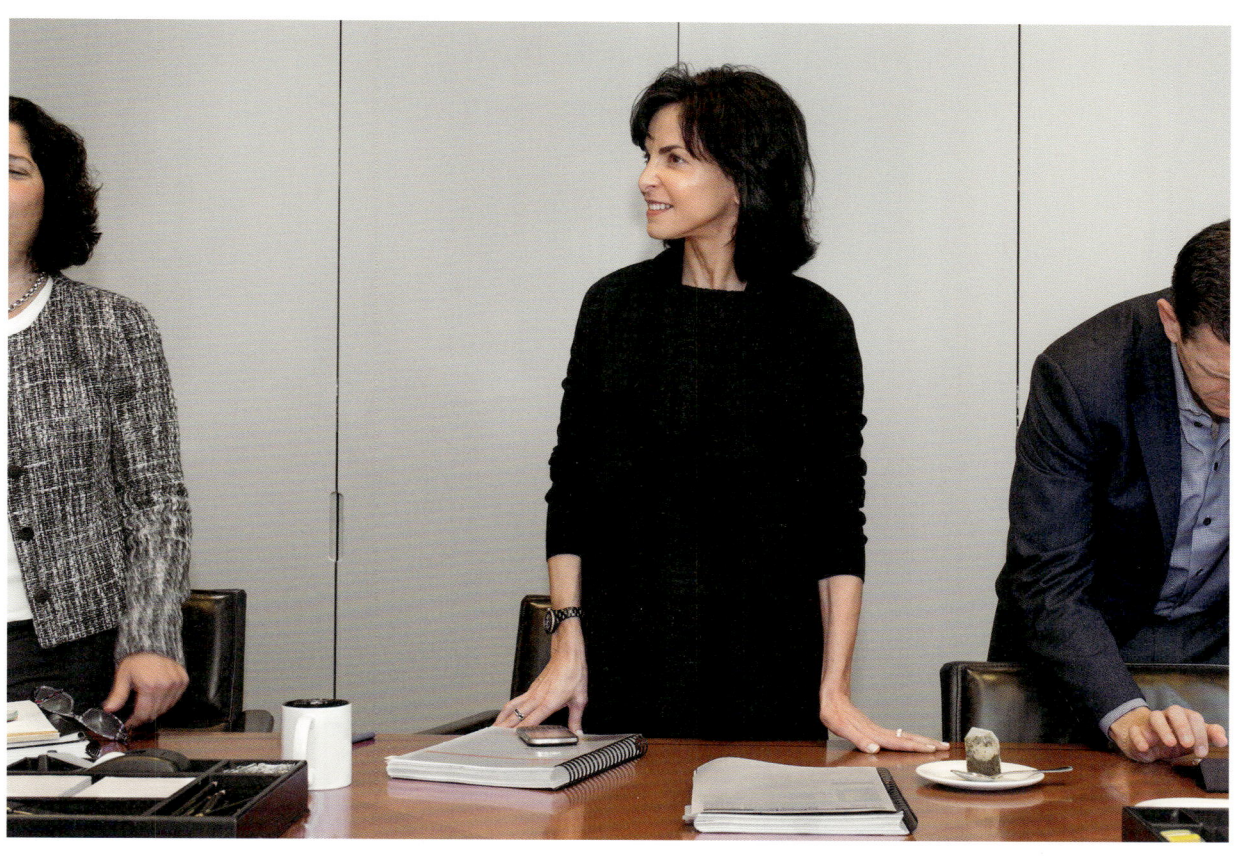

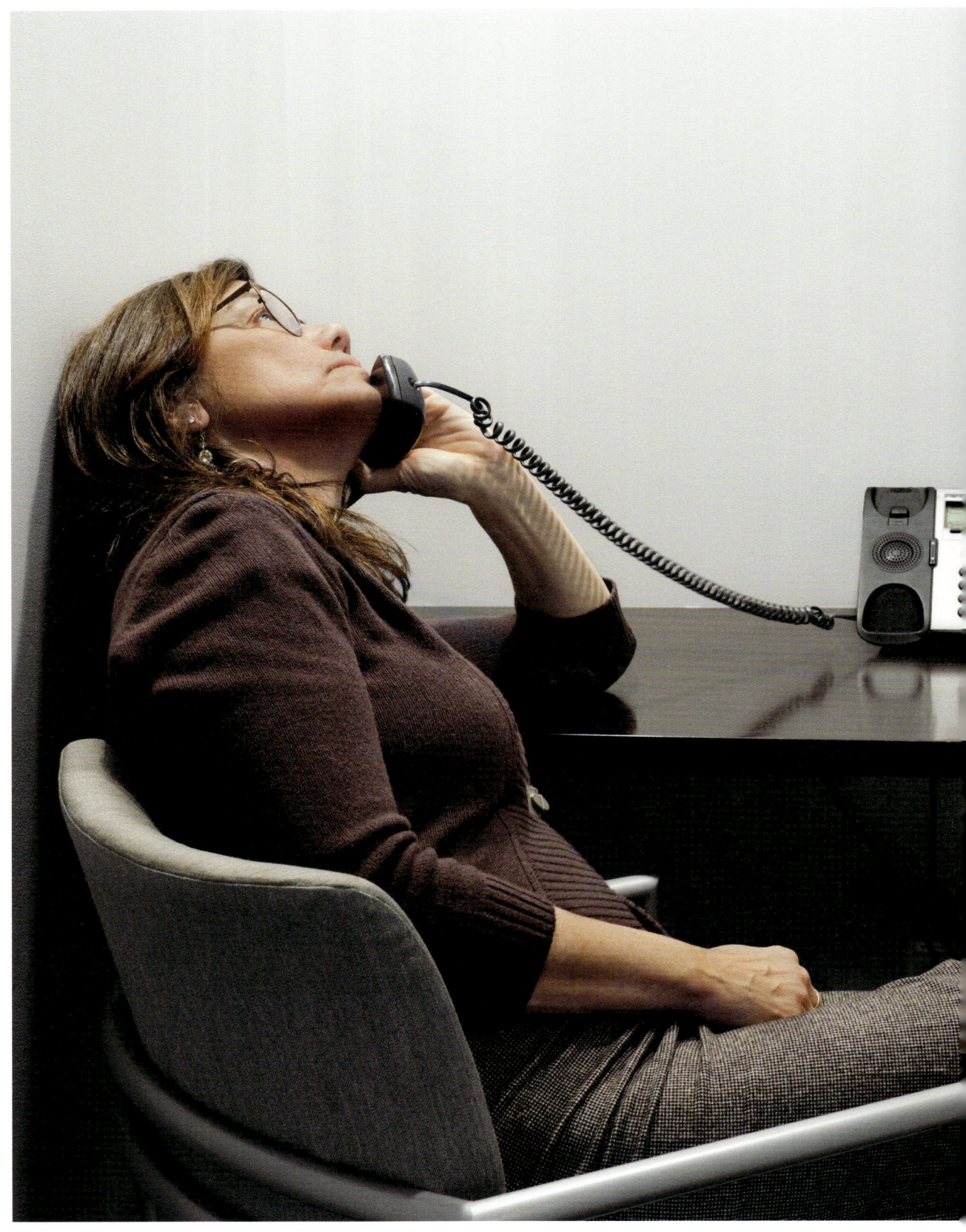

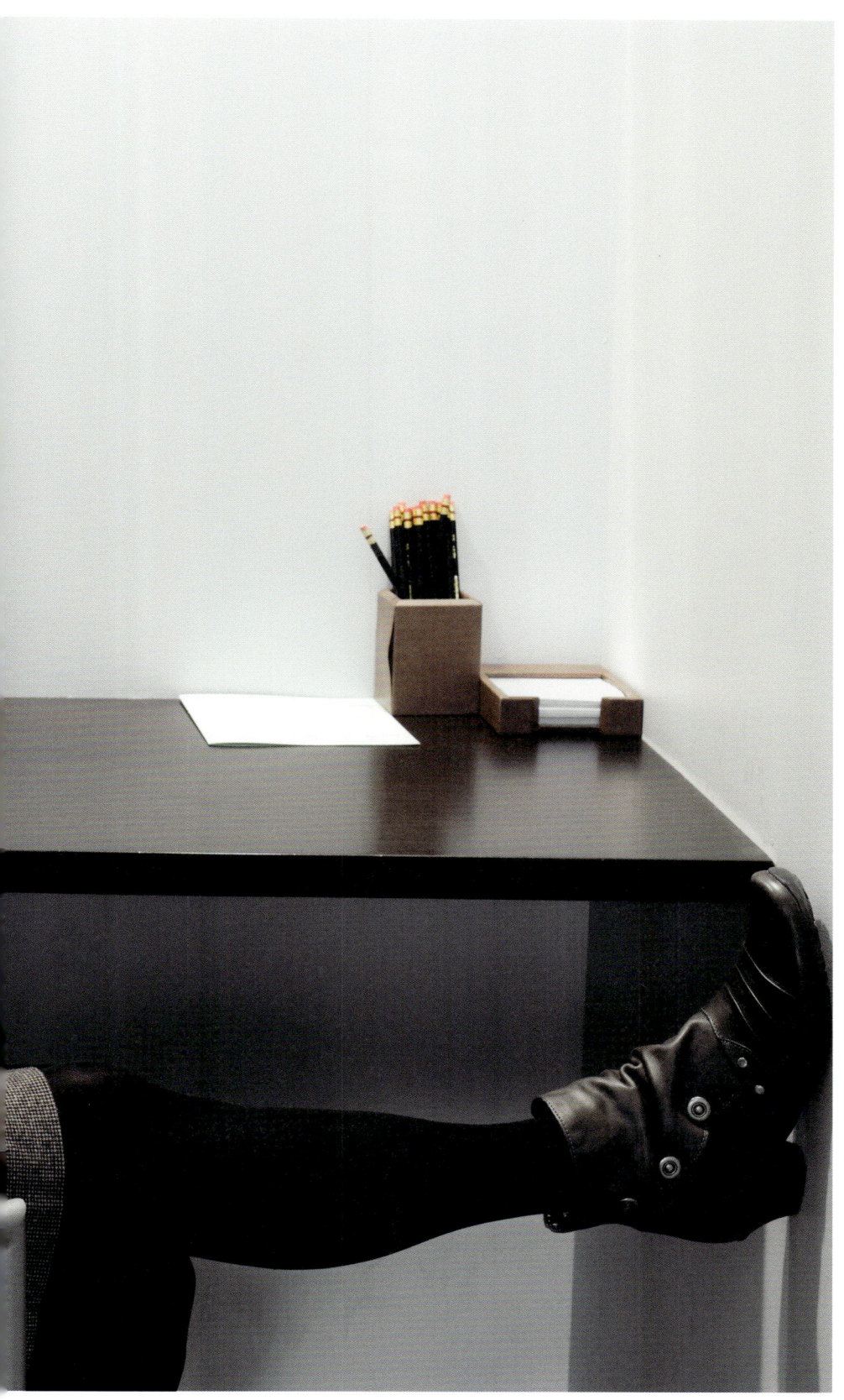

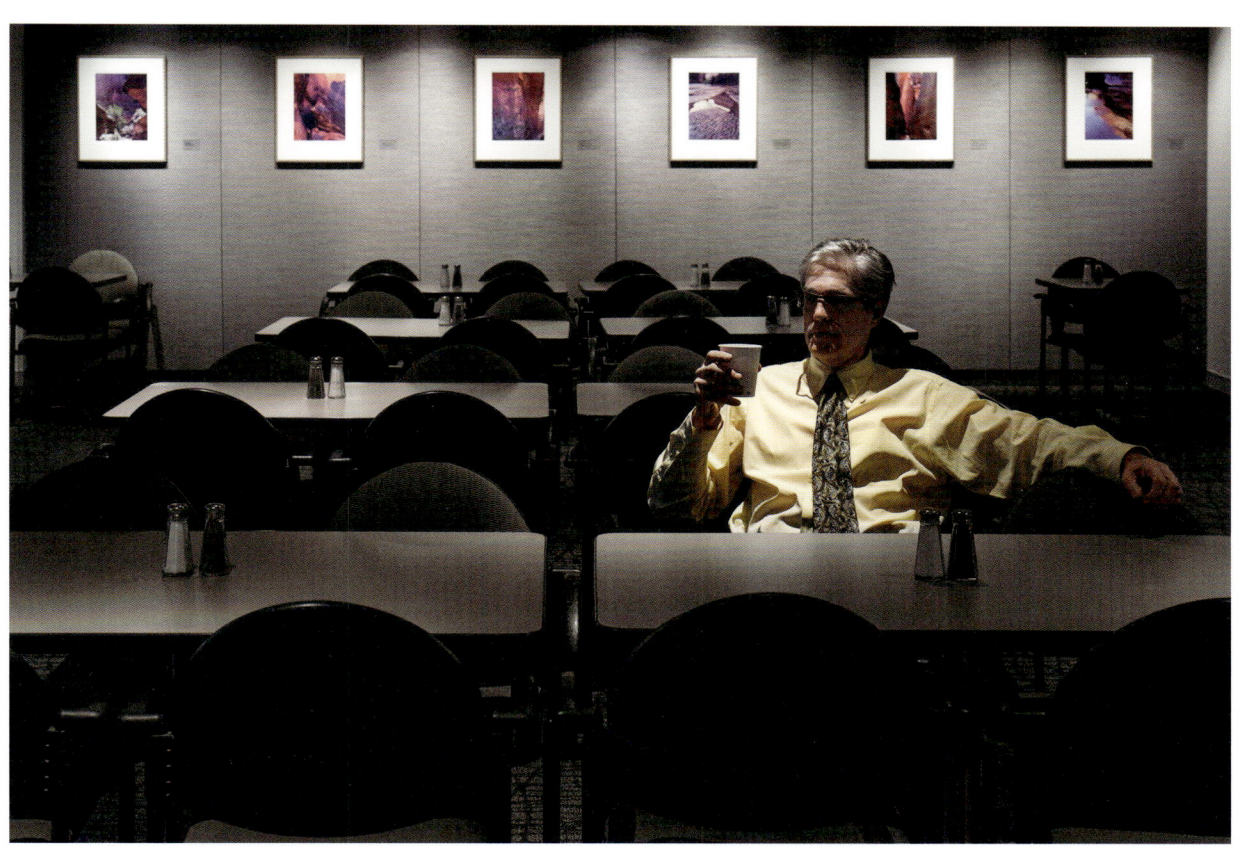

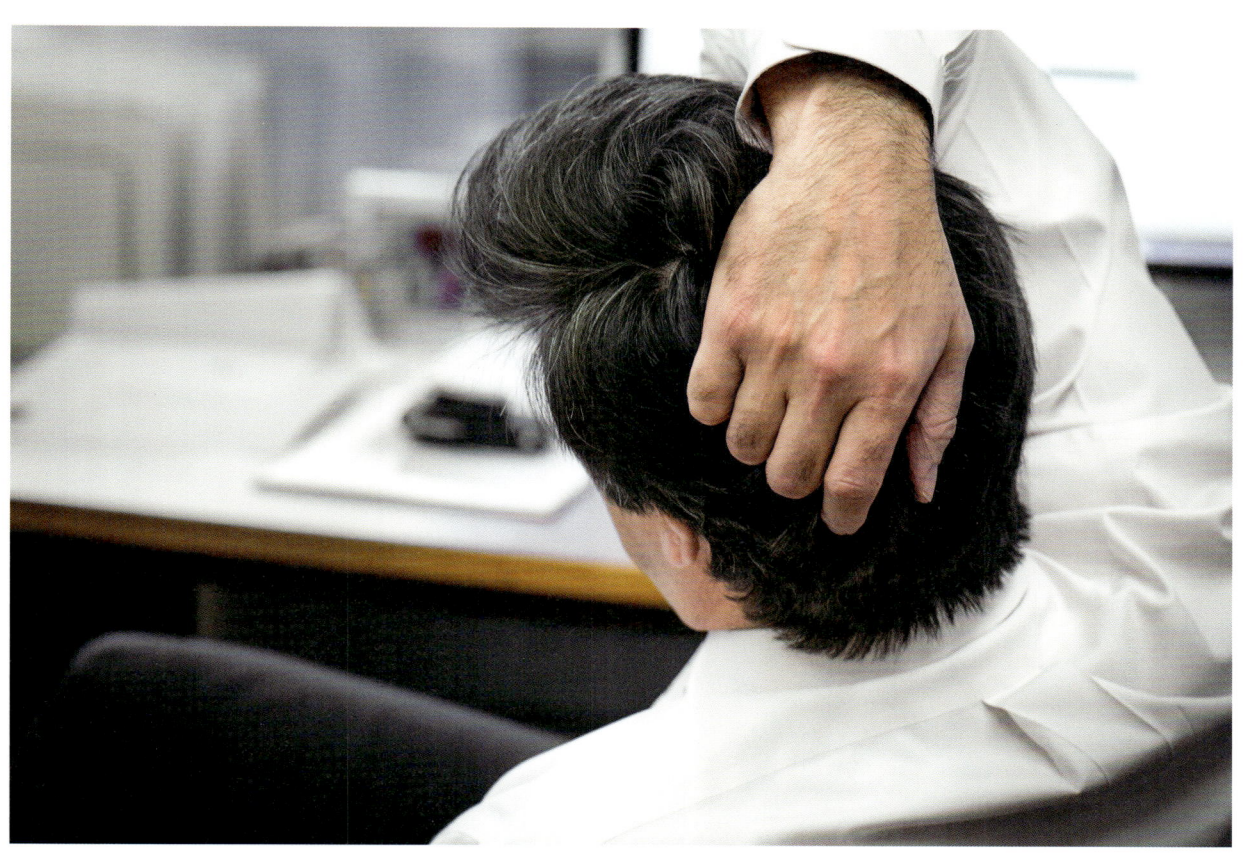

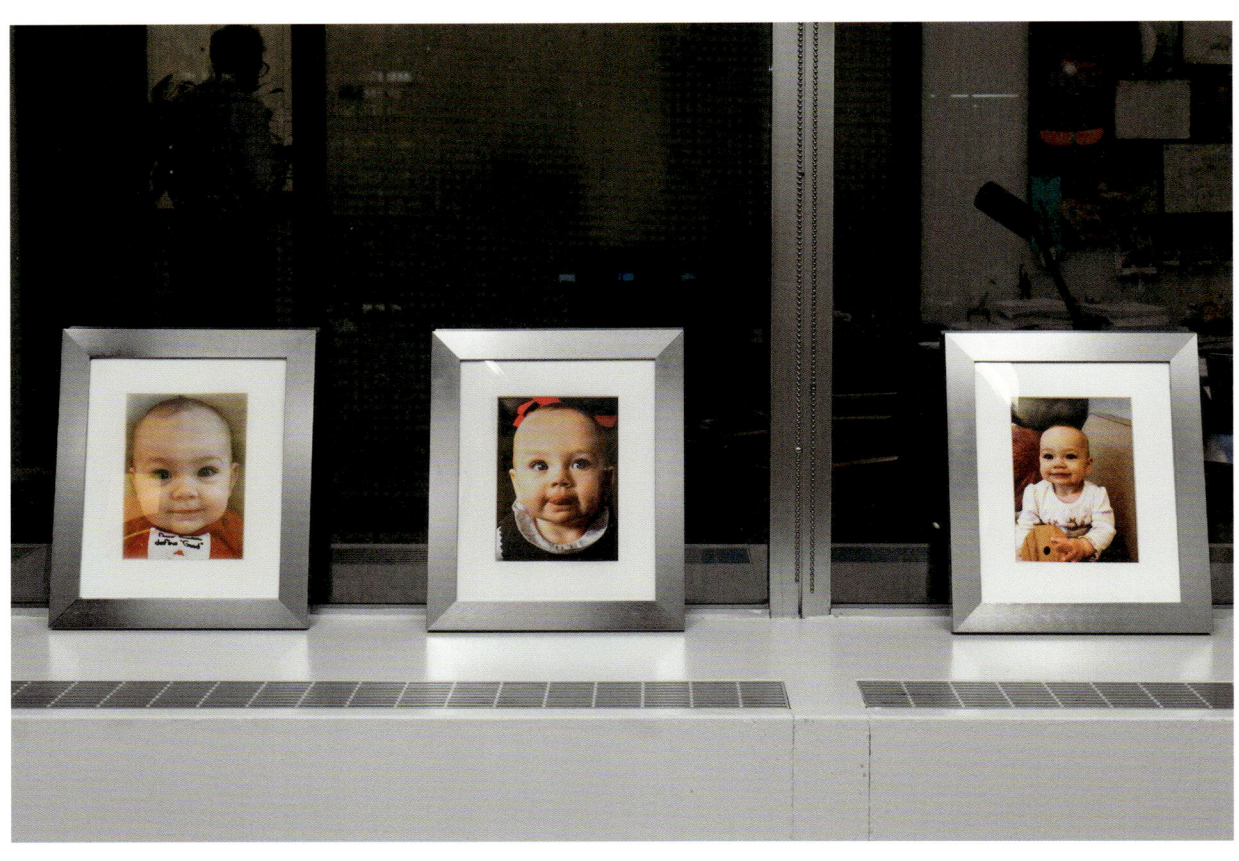

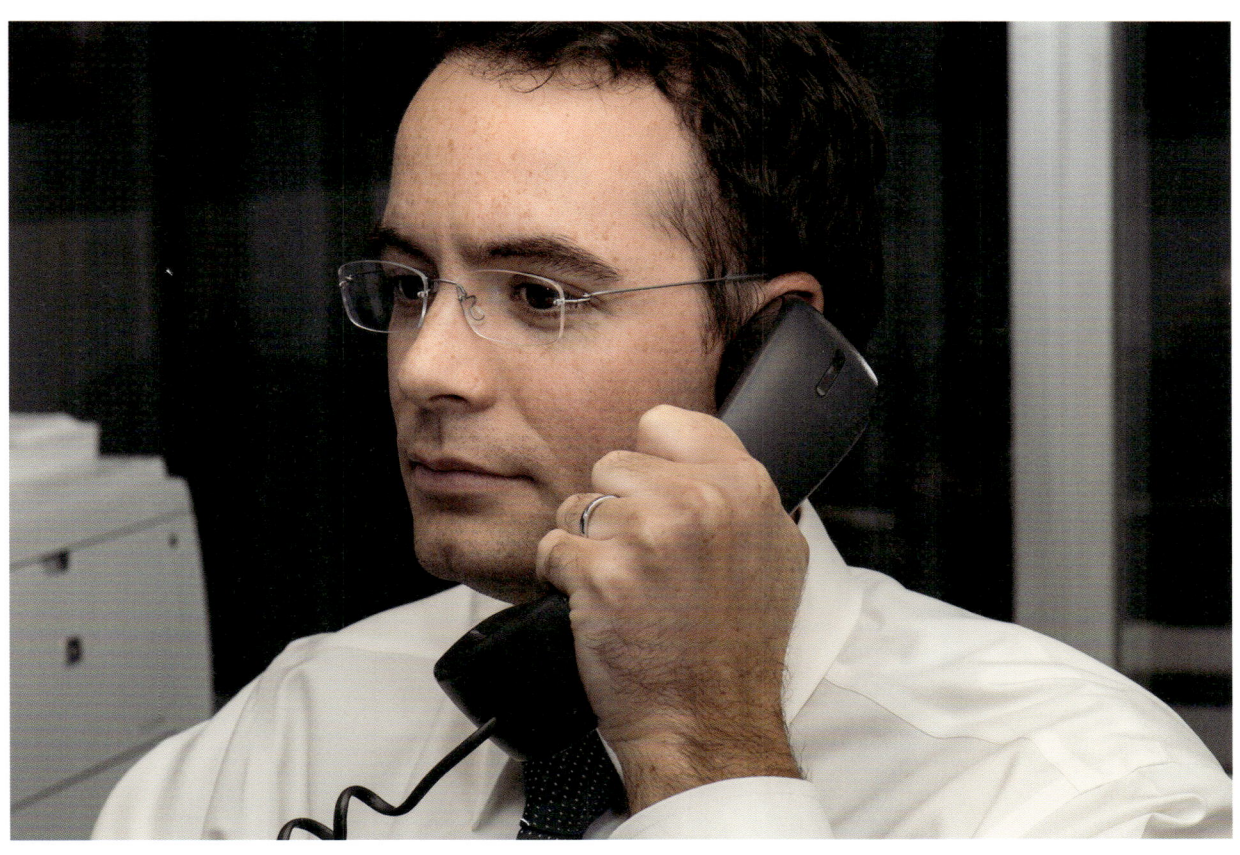

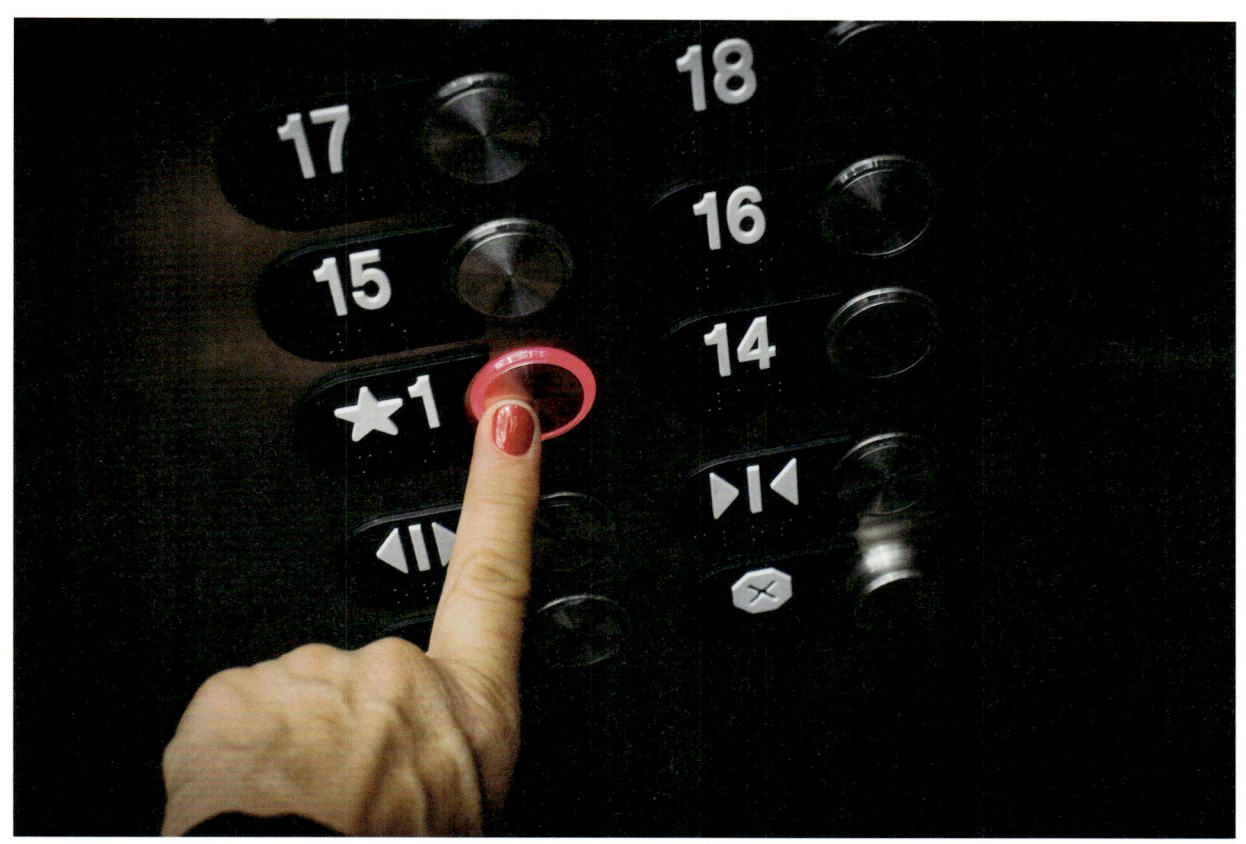

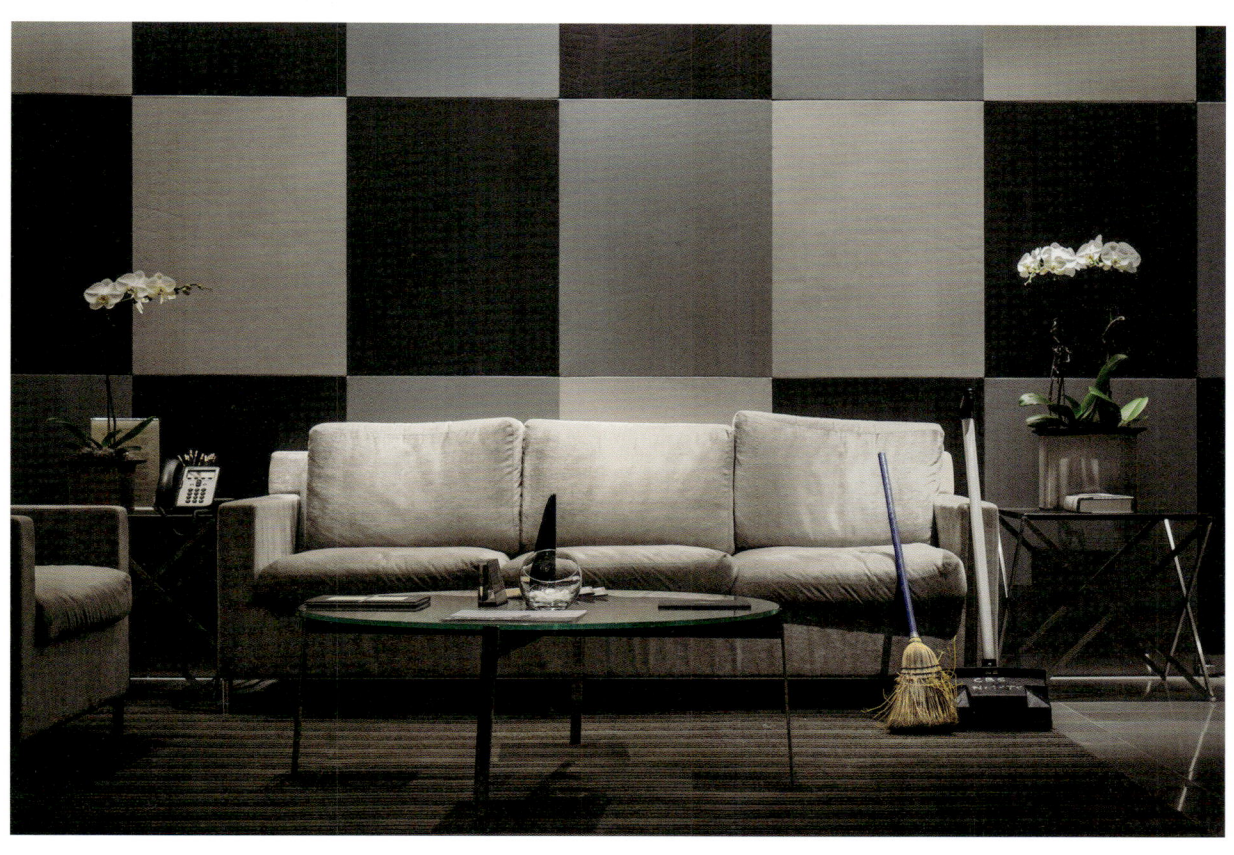

Robin Dahlberg's *Billable Hours* and the Hidden Cost of Women's Work

The #MeToo movement cast a new light on the old problem of sexual discrimination and harassment. As the hashtag #MeToo was shared 12 million times on social media during two days in October 2017, many men asked their wives, mothers, friends, and daughters if things were really that bad, and, if they were, why couldn't they see it? Robin Dahlberg's *Billable Hours* offers an answer to that question and opens up a new perspective on how gender discrimination and sexual harassment hide in plain sight.

Dahlberg's staged photographs are set in the world of corporate law. Here, men have always been in charge and their presence at the center is invisible to them. Groups of blue-shirted, red-tied men surround the women in Dahlberg's images. Men have a master-of-the-universe confidence, while women look wary, on guard, and exhausted. It is clear women are doing more work. More psychological and emotional work is required of women in male-dominated spaces, including the invisible and unpaid labor that Dahlberg's images record.

Billable Hours also reflects on the pressures that women face at the end of the workday, including the division of labor around childcare and housework that feminist sociologists call the "second shift." During the early months of the coronavirus pandemic, for example, men did more than they had done previously, but they overestimated how much they contributed. Nearly half of men said they did most of the home schooling, with some saying they did almost all of it. Guess what women said? About 3 percent agreed with that assessment.[1]

Dahlberg asks us to look again at the world of corporate law and to see how power hides in everyday routines. Caught between the demand to stand out and blend in, and pressured to adopt a gendered uniform of power in the form of stiletto heels, women are forced into a balancing act with no net to catch them. In an especially apt image, we see a woman's legs sprawled on the ground and a spilled array of pencils. It's a visual punchline to the exhortation to "lean in!" When women do, where are the structures to support them? The kind men rely on to succeed, access through privilege, and scarcely notice.

Billable Hours offers a way to see power and privilege in the space of a corporate law practice. Dahlberg's photographs enable us to see better what is hiding in plain sight and to ask: How can men learn to see their privilege and relinquish some of it? How can all of us see the invisible work women do and accurately value it? Life is not parceled out in billable hours, but Dahlberg invites us to think about what hostile environments cost women in terms of daily wear and tear. She asks us to see the toll women are expected to pay.

Leigh Gilmore
Author of *Tainted Witness: Why We Doubt What Women Say About Their Lives*
Visiting Professor of English, The Ohio State University

---

1 https://www.nytimes.com/2020/05/06/upshot/pandemic-chores-homeschooling-gender.html.

Photos Vérité: At the Big Law Firm

Robin Dahlberg's intriguing photos stoke memories.

I began law school in 1958. There were three other women in my section of the first-year class, and about eight in my graduating class. Institutionally, women were not unwelcome in my law school, but, pervasively, women were the brunt of jokes. In some classes, professors simply did not call on women. In one class, the professor allowed women to speak only on "Ladies' Day."

In my second year of law school, my classmates and I looked for summer jobs in law firms. At that time, an applicant simply went to the law offices, presented a resume to the receptionist, who gave it to a hiring partner, and was interviewed. I went to Wall Street (then home to all of the big law firms) one day after classes. A representative of the first firm I visited said the firm did not hire women; its summer program was for young men likely to join the firm after law school graduation and vie to become partner. I heard the same message everywhere else I went.

Meanwhile, law school was challenging and wonderful. I was a devoted student and loved my studies. I was a member of the law review and fondly remember the collegiality, the late-night sessions, and the shared academic community. I was not critical of the status of women. I was grateful to have the chance to participate in the great learning of the law.

In my third year of law school, I thought seriously about my career. My horizons were not broad. I had heard that some firms hired women in their tax departments, and some for trusts and estates. I knew that if I did not get a job with a law firm, I could get a job with a legal publisher. Because I was pregnant in my last year of law school, I postponed my law firm search.

I graduated, took the bar examination, and did research for a professor at the law school. In November 1961, I gave birth to my first child. In January 1962, I hired a babysitter for four hours and left the apartment with a list of the names and addresses of the big Wall Street law firms sent to me at my request by my law school's placement office. I went to the law firm that was located nearest to the subway exit, since time was of the essence—I had to get back to nurse my baby. Almost immediately, the firm offered me the lowly job of searching files in the office of a client to identify documents requested by the government for possible evidence in a major antitrust case. The case itself was interesting; it was in the media industry and involved major movie studios. Additionally, I knew that the law firms generally were not hiring women, and this was an opportunity. I accepted the offer. I stayed on for the next fourteen years, and in 1970, I became the firm's first woman partner.

To the extent that my professional life just happened to me, I was fortunate beyond belief. My law firm was a most remarkable one. Its senior partner was Whitney North Seymour, a leader of the bar in every sense and a model of the humanistic, socially concerned, humane, renaissance lawyer. A towering figure, he wore a bowler hat in winter and a boater in summer. Photographs of United States Supreme Court Justices lined his office wall. They were personally signed by the Justices, to Whitney, "with regard."

Whitney's office was at the end of a long corridor lined by a green carpet. When I walked down that green carpet and came to Whitney's office door, he would say to me, as he said to others, "Good morning, counselor. Come on in and put your feet up." And we would talk about a case I was working on with him, and the majesty of the law.

In 1963, the year after I began to practice law, women comprised only 3.8 percent of all incoming law students. Only one other woman associate was then employed by my firm, and she left soon after my arrival. By 1970, women comprised 8.5 percent of incoming law students; 5.1 percent of law firm associates were women. When I became a partner in the law firm on January 1, 1970, apparently only two other women were or had ever been partners at major Wall Street law firms.

In the 1970s, women began visibly to assert their rights, in law firms as well as in law schools. Almost suddenly, women were hired in not insignificant numbers, and women began to be invited to annual law firm outings. Occasionally, discrimination suits were brought against Wall Street law firms. One such suit was settled by a consent decree requiring affirmative efforts in hiring and promoting women.

I left my law firm to become a law professor in 1976. Not long thereafter, more than 40 percent of the new graduates of law schools were women. Today, women comprise about 50 percent. Many young lawyers are contemplating professional lives harmonious with personal lives, yet the firms are demanding more and more billable hours from each associate. There is no more luxury to learn the law at the feet of the great people of the profession. The age of the renaissance lawyer has passed, though there are always exceptions we can praise. The partners, and especially senior partners, continue to be disproportionately male, and women partners continue to report that they hit the "glass ceiling." In 2018, fewer than 20 percent of law firm equity partners were women. Female lawyers, including partners, earned about one-third less than their male counterparts.*

However, there is still hope. We have our heroes. I write this essay two days after the sad passing of illustrious Supreme Court Justice Ruth Bader Ginsburg, who fortunately was able to see her path in life go from anomaly to possibility for younger generations of women.

Robin Dahlberg's photos tell a lot of the story. They are starkly realistic. They document attitude. They document power: who has it and who doesn't. They document the pressures to conform on those at the low rungs of the ladder. They document the unsung hard work, long hours, devotion, and sometimes frenzy of those who have to work harder than the men, without complaint, to even hope to get to the same place or just to keep their job. In their witty way, Robin's photos say much more than words could do.

Eleanor M. Fox
Walter J. Derenberg Professor of Trade Regulation
New York University School of Law

A portion of this essay was excerpted from "Being a Women, Being a Lawyer and Being a Human Being—Women and Change," Fordham Law Review, Vol. 57, Issue 6, 1989, by Eleanor M. Fox.

*Wulfhorst, Ellen. "Gender pay gap is dramatic among top U.S. lawyers, survey finds," December 6, 2018, Reuters, https://www.reuters.com/article/us-usa-women-pay/gender-pay-gap-is-dramatic-among-top-us-lawyers-finds-idUSKBN1O52JL; Cassens Weiss, Debra. "Full-time female lawyers earn 77 percent of male lawyer pay," ABA Journal, March 17, 2016, https://www.abajournal.com/news/article/pay_gap_is_greatest_in_legal_occupations.

Acknowledgments

Thank you to that big Los Angeles-based law firm for which I worked when I first graduated from law school and which served as an inspiration for this project. (You know who you are.)

Thank you to my lawyer-husband, Ted Maynard, for his endless support and facilitation of this project.

Thank you to Jörg Colberg who first suggested that I do a photo project on being a lawyer.

Thank you to the Daylight Community Arts Foundation for providing a larger platform for my photography.

And thank you to my son, Hayden Maynard, whose creativity and courage inspire me daily.